A REASON TO *Live*

CHERYL D. SANFORD

ISBN 978-0-578-74256-4

Introduction

As we walk through the journey of life, we wear many faces. For some of us, this is a n easy task. Life seems to roll along quite well, without disruption and with abundant rewards. Whereas, for other individuals, it is not that simplified. There is hardship, turmoil, and pain to last several lifetimes.

There are many different origins of people in this wonderful world that we live in. Even though we all seem to be fabricated the same, we are all unique and respond to life's ups and downs in our own special way. For how "we" perceive life is not how "others" see it.

In this book, you will read of my personal experiences, good and bad.

Some of the material written may not be suitable for some. If you can keep an open mind, I will share my story. It will take you through an incredible journey. It is a story of childhood happiness, hopes and dreams, and growing pains. It is a story of depression, suffering, and addiction, as well as death. But I will also share with you a story of strength, hope, recovery, and acceptance. I am confident that upon reading this lifetime autobiography, your life will be changed dramatically. You will find encouragement, motivation, strength, love, and hope.

I used to accept life as it was and blamed others for my actions.

I have hit many bottoms in life and have indeed seen "hell on earth." I have lost my faith numerous times throughout my lifetime. However, through all the struggle and diversity, I have been taught precious lessons. Learning from my mistakes, I have learned how, through my Higher Power, to live my life as it was intended. I have learned how to take all the negative influences around me, and live life with meaningful purpose.

I have suffered many losses in a lifetime. People that I have admired and have dearly loved. There have numerous evictions, homes lost, cars repossessed, and personal material items lost forever. But, through these dramatizing times, there seemed to always be some type of divine intervention. It seemed to always be there, even if it was a tiny thread holding me up.

I have come from a world of guilt, remorse, self-hatred, and loss of power in my life. Today, I love and respect myself. I have empathy and love for others, as well as the world around me. Today, I try extremely hard not to judge others, and except those around me, as they were created. I have learned to express myself without pride and anger. I have learned that the only boundaries that I have are the ones that I set for myself. Nothing is impossible. The goals that I have set for myself, and the accomplishments that have been obtained today, well, they are nothing short of small miracles.

I do believe that we are the holders of our own destiny. We all have the power of free will. But choices today will affect our lives tomorrow, and for the rest of our lives.

These decisions will also bear a consequence on our loved ones, friends, acquaintances, and even strangers. Even the world shall inherit our mistakes.

Personally, spiritual guidance is recommended. For me, I would not be here today without it. I am not a doctor, minister, scholar, scientist, nor the professor of any sort.

I am just like you. Although some of you may take occupation in some of these fields. I wanted to attend medical school to become a "Brain Surgeon" (Rocket Science classes were filled). That was a joke. If anyone falls in that category, that was a compliment! But this is my real-life story. I hope this book will create an everlasting impact on your life and the people that surround you. Keep whatever you want and be inspired. Throw what you do not need or have any use for, away. Also, I wanted to add that I have changed some of the names of individuals. This was done respectfully to protect their privacy. However, the towns and incidents happened as honestly and truthfully that I have remembered.

Enjoy the book

It has taken me many years, many tears, and an intense look into my life, to recall a lot of memories. There have been unforeseen obstacles that have prevented me from finishing it. The necessity and the desire to share this was worth the time. It has opened up an even greater strength and peace inside, that I never knew existed.

INNOCENT BEGINNINGS

I was born in Cheverly, Maryland, in the wonderful year of 1963.

I say this because; it was the period of my life that will always be the most precious to me. This was a very historic year. It was on a Friday, November 22, that our most beloved President, JFK, was shot in Dallas, Texas. He was traveling with his wife, Jacqueline and Governor John Connally, and his wife in a presidential motorcade, at the time of the event. He was assassinated at 12:30 pm, in Dealey Plaza.

The investigation from November 1963 to September 1964 concluded that Lee Harvey Oswald, acting alone, was the sniper. Jack Ruby killed Oswald before he could stand trial. The Warren Commission also stated that he also worked alone. In later years, of course, these findings have been proven controversial. They have been challenged and supported by the following studies. This was when Vice President Lyndon B. Johnson took over as 36th President. His vision was to build "A Great Society" for the American people.

Times were simple, pleasant, and slow-paced in the late '60s.

Not like the 2000s, where we almost solely rely on computers for everything. It seems as if we are always in a hurry to get nowhere. The earliest childhood memory was when I was four years old.

I remember visiting my Grandmother, located in Bealeton, Virginia. It possessed all the traits of the typical southern Virginia homes that were way before "my" time. There was a long unpaved road that was not recognizable from the main road. It was two stories, with gray unpainted wood, and an outhouse for specific personal relief. I was so small and terrified of falling in that hole. This is also the time when I had my very brief encounter with the neighbor's goat. A little hint; never turn your back up against a fence when there is a goat around. My buttocks still remember the pain of those two small horns stabbing into them! Even to this day, I tend to watch my back in "Petting Farms."

I try to avoid them at all costs.

I even remember our gold rush adventures in the ditch near the house. I found out later it was sedimentary rocks, like a limestone. I do not have too many more accurate memories of this era, because, I again, was still at a very young age.

PRACTICAL PARENTS

My parents were truly the most incredible people that you could ever know. My childhood was far from dysfunctional. My family was not wealthy, but the quality of life that was maintained for us was extremely suitable. We never really wanted for anything, nor did we desire more than what we had. Our home life was fulfilling and comfortable. The house was isolated away from neighbors, but always safe and secure. Accept when the next-door neighbor's cows decided to break through the dilapidated wire fence and furnish the grass with free excrement droppings. Later in life, Dad wanted to educate my children and me to witness the miraculous birth of one of these creatures. It was a breech birth. The baby calf was up and standing in just a few minutes. It was one of the most grotesque visions that I have ever experienced in my life. Not for the weak-hearted.

We always had food on the table. Dad generated a one-acre vegetable garden. My father appointed me as his helper when I was around age five.

He taught me how to generate a garden by hand and how to drive and use the tractor for proper productivity.

It was also learned at age six, how to break my leg on the tractor. It was an accident. I believe my mother had blamed him. Primarily, I was not paying attention to where I was placing my feet. My father incorporated responsibility and hard work in me at this time. However, I did not know this at the time. Sometimes, it is hard for us to understand the motives when we are very young.

My Dad was a good man and loved his family very much. He knew how to work his "fingers to the bone" literally. He was born the year 1922, in Washington DC. As we all know, that was during "The Depression," so he was from a generation that took nothing for granted. Warren G. Harding, the 29th President was residing at that time. My father demonstrated firmness in making decisions. He also could effectively influence critical decision-makers. This is why he went from being a projectionist in theatres to becoming delegated as the Business Agent for a local in Washington, DC, for many years. He was always supported by his convictions with sufficient force. However, his self-discipline was lacking at times when it came to expressing his feelings. I believe he was just overworked. He did not do too badly for a farm boy with a third-grade education.

My mother was a very kind, gentle, and quiet individual. She was born in the year 1932. This was when Herbert Hoover was residing as President.

She had grown up in Southern Virginia.

She moved to Northern Virginia when she was eighteen. She got an apartment and immediately started to work for C&P Telephone Company.

Much later, she had retired from there also. She could analyze conditions and reach independent decisions. My father had to be at his office quite a lot. She had to be the administrator at home.

CHERISHED CHILDHOOD

Back during the '60s and '70s, women had the luxury of staying at home and raising children. My mother stayed focused on initiating and establishing personal growth and development with my brother and myself. She was very committed and dedicated to this responsibility. I have a lot of admiration for my Mom for doing this for us.

As, well as for any one individual, male or female that takes on this sound decision. It was not until later in life, when I had my children, did I appreciate what she had sacrificed. Again, if I could go back in time, I would take that switch off the tree, and beat my buttocks with it. It is so funny when we are young that we take so many things for granted.

We do not understand objectives fully until we get older.

When I was a child, I was always protected and cared for. It breaks my heart to see children now, who have not lived a childhood as such. You can tell in a child's eyes when they are not cared for. I am blessed to have the ability to have empathy for others. At least now, I do. Every one of God's creatures deserves that individualized care.

Growing up in the late '60s and early '70s were unbelievable.

We had the "flower power" styled bell-bottom pants, long butterfly winged blouses and stacks. You know, "the old high heeled shoes." I do believe that they are back in style again.

The boys had longer hair than the girls back then. I even recall our first color T.V. Dad had to go outside on the roof, whenever we had a storm. The antenna had to be manually adjusted to get the perception back again. My two favorite toys were a slinky and a hobby horse. Toys "R" Us was not established at that time. I had a lot of pots and pans to play with. Going to the library, borrowing books and reading was greatly encouraged weekly by my mother. My Mom enforced this skill at an early age. In my later years growing up the adjoining woods became my playground.

I will never forget the time when my father told me to go outside and "look for a needle in the haystack." For hours, and months I looked every day one summer and could not find it. It took me a few seasons to figure out why my Dad had that grin on his face every time I walked through the door, disappointed. I'm glad someone got a laugh at my expense. Luckily, for my Dad, I had a sense of humor back then.

We watched a lot of television back in those days. Some of my favorite television programs were "The Monkees," "The Brady Bunch," and "The Wonderful World of Disney." At an early age, I entertained myself with my mother's manually operated typewriter. From this, I learned the importance of accuracy. You had to avoid making mistakes and errors, though. My mother never seemed to have a bottle of Liquid Paper around. It was invented in 1951 by Bette Nesmith Graham, also the mother of musician and producer Michael Nesmith of The Monkees. As I recall, my administrative skills needed to be developed.

Back in those days, I had my collection of stuffed animals.

They were my only friends; they were my companions and were also my receptive audience for my theatrical plays.

My, how they applauded when I used my creative strength to conduct my one-person shows. Judging by their enthusiasm, I don't think they got out too much. As a child, I demonstrated I high degree of originality, and creativity. Besides, I had to keep them around. They diligently and affectively kept the monsters in the closet and out of my bedroom. There were names for all of my stuffed friends, but my favorite was "Snowbear."

He was a small Panda Bear and he went with me everywhere. When I was a child, I was hyper, imaginative, and spontaneous. Life was beautiful to me. I saw the world as a fun place, untouched by any evil. Invincible was my middle name, and I was capable of doing anything. Trying my parents' patients seemed to be my greatest achievement.

In the summertime, we always had large and spectacular family reunions. Now that I am older, I miss those days. All of my Aunts and Uncles from both sides of my family have passed on.

Only great memories remain instilled in my heart. The holidays were always spectacular. Christmas was my most adored time of year. Our house was abundantly filled with lights and decorations. Except for the one year our German Sheppard, "Grant," ate the light bulbs. He went psycho after that. The poor dog went after a neighbor's pony and we had to have him put down. I guess you are never really the same after an ordeal like that. Children's parties were always a blast. "Pin the Tail on the Donkey" was my favorite game. I always won, well, I always peeked too. Mom always went all out for special occasions.

PRE-TEEN AWAKENING

As I entered the pre-teen era, my favorite pastime was listening to my "own" music, on my "own" record player. Trying to establish a connection with my fathers' obsession with "The Lawrence Welk Show" and "Hee Haw" every Sunday as a child was starting to stunt my growth. I learned to display the ability to adapt to my surroundings at an early age.

Besides, they were the only shows that came on before Disney. My music style at this time consisted of primarily one group. The "DeFranco Family," with Tony DeFranco, was the absolute center of my universe. My bedroom clearly stated that I was hopelessly obsessed and infatuated with this kid. In 1973, when his number 1# hit was released, "Heartbeat, It's a love beat," I immediately begged my mother, too, buy it for me. I brought the 45 home, and yes we had 45's back then, now they are called vinyls. It is a miracle that my mother still has all the hair because I must have played that record over a thousand times in a day. You are talking about an extreme case of compulsive behavior. I believe this was when I needed a severe behavior modification. This display of enthusiasm was present for months. My Mom got fed up with buying needles for the player.

As a few seasons past, my parents presented me with a used organ.

My mother sat down and showed me the correct way to place my fingers and hands. I watched her and then sat and proceeded to play. To my surprise, I seemed to display the ability to play by ear.

Later in middle school, I also learned to play the Clarinet, as well as classes to read music. However, my ambition lacked the intense involvement that it took to achieve results for future success in that field. Okay, I was lazy. The commitment was not desirable at the time. Besides, I wanted to be a comedian like "Lucille Ball." An actor who consistently exceeded performance expectations! She always had a way of being resourceful beyond means.

During my early school years, my brother and I went to a private Christian School. The curriculum was strict, and they seemed to excel in achieving perfection for all their students. You were expected to conform to appropriate dress codes. You were expected to be assertive without being aggressive. When we had Sunday school, it was positive at the first impression. When the preacher started yelling and screaming and telling us that all of us sinners was going to Hell to burn forever, well, let's just say, that had a terrifying image left in my little child mind. At this time of my life, my understanding of God was a God of hate, anger, judgment, and fear. I tried so hard to make my parents happy that I started neglecting to have fun for myself. It was almost like I was a puppet on a string. I learned a lot, education-wise; however, the obsessive nature of this type of religion started to freak me out a little. I didn't believe that God hated me so much. Apart from that, I would have to say that my childhood was the happiest time of my life. However, that perfect and sound environment was about to take a little leap into puberty. This is where my friend, the real fun started.

GROWING PAINS

So here I am at the ripe old age of 13, going on 30. It was at this time that I believed I was an adult. All teenagers think the same, as finding out in later years. However, for me, at the time, my confidence and self-esteem were at a weakening level.

Watching television, listening to music, and chilling out in my bedroom, was all the responsibility that I desired.

My undying love for movies as still not ceased. It was around this time that I got to see my first R-rated movie. After a lot of ineffective begging, my mom gave in and took me to see "The Exorcist." The movie came out in 1973, but it took a while for her to take me to see it.

Still, to the day, scares the Hell out of me! Living only a short distance away from where they filmed the house and stairs, I got to go there. The experience was too surreal. A lady bumped into my shoulder by accident, as I was looking down the steps. I ran back to the car. This incident happened when I was in my forties.

I cried all the way home.

Roller skating was the only outside recreation that I enjoyed, other than swimming in the summer at the local high school. Back then, in my town, that was all we had unlike today, where technology has replaced social resources. We played football, baseball, tennis, and badminton in the back yard. These kids now just use their computer resources.

Our family did, however, spend numerous times at the Drive-in. My Dad worked at several establishments; therefore, I used resources for our unlimited admittance. The special treatment made me feel like a VIP, and of course, I liked the attention.

We had a German Sheppard named Grant. My brother and I used to ride him when we were younger. Getting older, I wanted the responsibility to have my own dog. He was a small, pudgy, black mutt. For the first time, I had significant responsibility for another living being.

This seemed like a new beginning of happiness for me. My willingness to please my parents and excel in school again was strengthened.

I was happy again, just like a child.

As I was trying very hard to regain my family's trust, school life was about the same. Peer pressure can be hard to tolerate, as a child and as an adult. Trying to keep everyone else happy, I spared my own But my new companion and friend made life tolerable.

One day, it was raining real hard outside. My dog was not allowed in the house, but the weather was so bad that I begged my mom to let him come in. I called for him numerous times. There was no response. Proceeding up to the road, I could barely see in front of me. The rain was impairing my vision to see beyond a few feet. I wanted to find Blackie! Where was my dog! I called his name several times and no answer. I thought to myself, if something happened to my friend, I don't know what I would do. Panic came over me. When I was getting ready to give up, there was a bag on the side of the road, being aggressively curious; I wanted to see what treasures it contained. My search for the dog halted. Heading closer to the bag, I looked down to pick it up. It was Blackie. He had been run over by a car. He was dead.

We buried Blackie the next day. My heart was broken. My inability to handle emotional disappointments was lacking at this time.

The world around me had shattered into pieces. I blamed God for killing him. The blame and guilt that was put on my parents by me were there too. For weeks, I cried, and stayed in my room, as always.

When I was alone, I was safe from the world. When I finally got over my tantrum, sitting down at dinner, I apologized. So then, with my pleasant and cheerful disposition, "when can I get another dog"?

Life went on after that, as it always does. Roller skating became my all-time favorite past time. In the summer, I was allowed to go several times a week with such enthusiasm for the sport. This is where I found my other favorite pastimes, 'boys'.

Developing into a young woman at an early age seemed to be a positive magnetism at this time. Looking back, I should have stayed in my room and studied more.

The boys usually stayed in one area in the back and played arcade and pinball games. Remember, the ones you put a quarter in for three games. Everyone who went there was around the ages of 12 to 16, so I hung out with kids a little older than myself. I had a fresh perception of life at this time. My solitude in my room was becoming of less importance to me. Getting the approval of my friends was. I just wanted to fit in.

Spending a lot of my summer nights at the rink was satisfying.

My friends, the few that I had, would meet me there. Smoking cigarettes was the most critical factor in being accepted as cool. So, of course, wanting to impress them, I took the risk and partook in this event. They did not tell me that 35 years later, still smoking, still coughing, and paying $7.50 for a pack of cigarettes, that the consequences of my actions would destroy my body. Back in those days, you could get a pack of cigarettes for 55 cents, from a machine.

By no means am I bragging. Some solid advice that I might have to my readers; if you smoke, please stop at any expense! If you have ever thought about smoking, even under the impact of stress, don't. I cannot express enough the dangerous outcome of the decision to do so. I cannot judge another human being; without it having affect my life, however, out of deep concern, please get the support system you need in this area.

A NEW AWAKENING

As my teenage years were running their course, I had a few crushes on some boys. There was nothing major, just your typical infatuations here and there. But for me, at the time, being a teenager, my hormones were actively evolving. Until one summer, at the age of 14, I met the love of my life. Having already lost my virginity at the age of 13, I thought I displayed a high degree of emotional security for a real relationship. We had a lot of fun together. For one summer, I had forgotten about the school, my parents, and myself. The objective of my life now was to make this person happy. At all expense to my personal needs and happiness, I tried with a spirit of determination.

A few months rolled by, nearing to the end of yet another summer.

Schools were formulating their plans to reopen. My enthusiasm to start a new year in another school was present. This time I was confident in myself. After all, I had my true love by my side supporting me. My attitude towards my parents had become warm and sincere. Mom and Dad got over the cigarette issue. They accepted it as "peer pressure". It was blamed on the other children. Well, I made it look like that. Trust was being maintained once again within my home life.

One day I was waiting around the house for my boyfriend to call.

Hours had gone by. The phone finally rang. Yeah! It was him. I conveyed my words of concern to him, making sure that he was alright. His brief words were as such; "we are breaking up". He hung up. What the "****"? Now, as an adult, one can most likely accept and cope effectively in conflicting relationships. But, being 14, I was unable to remain calm under that type of pressure. The feelings of betrayal and trust consumed me. I couldn't grasp any depth of understanding as to why this was happening. This was the end of the world for me. I truly wanted to die. I had given this person all the attention in the world and displayed unconditional love towards him. I had conformed myself to meeting his expectations and his needs. So now, this happens. I could not bear the agony of what I was feeling. Trying to maintain self-control, I barricaded myself in my room.

This time I could not find any resolution in doing so. A strong sense of uncontrolled anger was in me. I ran away. Honestly, I don't even remember where I went. My memory at that time seemed to have drawn a blank. It was the first of many episodes of running away.

When I got back home, I was not the same.

Anyhow, I liked the attention that I got. So I let the memories of him flee.

When I got back in school, I had a resistance to authority. Not following proper codes of conduct and keeping my anger under control were my greatest assets. Displaying emotional stability was a concern to my parents. For years, I went to several junior high schools. Being unable to adjust to any, and running away all the time, the alternative was a reform school. There were many of those, to be exact. This experience only heightened my resistance to change.

Somehow, the attention that I was receiving was giving me the strength of importance. After all, I was the "center of the universe." At least, that is what I believed at the time. I was comfortable will all my imperfections.

Besides, what did my parents know?

They were just two old people.

How could they understand how I feel?

How could anyone possibly understand me?

Even God had nothing to do with me.

I was alone. However, things were about to change.

INTO THE REAL WORLD

As I was becoming a pre-teen, my parents decided to take me out of the private school setting and place me into the public-school system. This shift in education techniques was tough on me. The sheltered and religious influenced life that I was used to, seems not to exist anymore.

Not in this world that I seemed to have been thrown into. There was a specific category of people that I was allowed to associate with. When growing up, and within the walls of the Christian School, I never heard the "GD" word. I still have a problem hearing it or saying it. Except, for one time, I fell off the monkey bars and got a paddling; but that hurt! Observing how different my classmates were from myself made it challenging to fit in. Observations of their mannerism and originality created a sense of curiosity.

My personal growth seemed to be slightly expanding. But still, the difficult, "new world" concept was hard to grasp. The memory skills of learning that I was accustomed to seeming to be irreverent here. It was almost like I had been demoted several grades. Comparing between the two, it was like, I was super smart, or these individuals had articulation issues. My basic perception of life at this time, I would have to say was slightly altered.

At home, around this time, family life was about the same as it had always been. Dad maintained his position at work, developing teamwork with his employees to optimize his subordinates' productivity. The proper recognition was never really given to him until later in life.

My father always displayed constant professionalism and pride in his work. As for this unique personality trait, he could not be home as much as he wanted to. My mother, and the other hand, had to take on full responsibility at home. She had small jobs that she periodically acquired; babysitting, ironing clothes for other women, etc. There was one kid that locked her outside one time. I thought my mother was going to lose it.

First time I think I ever heard her curse. Mom was very articulate, and foul language was not an option. She had an exceptional articulate vocabulary. I did not get out of the house that much in those days. My mother did not acquire a car, nor learn how to drive until around this time period.

Her first vehicle was a mid-60's Ford Comet. It was light brown, and it looked like a box. My mom, being only 5'3", had to poke her head up above the wheel, just to manage the car. The "Where's the Beef" commercial, with Clara Peller, that came out January 10, 1984, resembles this scenario. My brother and I used to call this "the rag car." Still, this day, I cannot get that image out of my mind.

It was at this age that I was starting to display and develop a strong sense of independence. Between eleven and twelve was a difficult time for me. Everything in my life, up until now, had the emotional security of my parents. My observation was that my mother had decided to allow me to learn self-reliance. I was allowed to express myself more in speaking occasions. I was timid then, but still had my extraordinary sparks of enthusiasm for life. So, I kept my verbal expressions to myself. There were times when I just had to be alone. Because when I did express myself, it seemed as though my thoughts and words could not connect. I had become so absorbed, with what I was "feeling," rather than what I was trying to communicate, that it just did not come out the way I meant it to. The reaction from my family was always the same; "sit down and shut up." The feelings that I had made my self-confidence soar downwards. Knowing what I was thinking and trying to explain it adequately was just impossible for me. So, I decided that if I had to communicate with anyone, it would be kept to a minimum. So, I kept mostly to myself.

Being alone, most of the time, really wasn't that bad. My bedroom demonstrated all the traits of a pre-teen. The floor had bright purple shag carpet, enhancing the lavender walls. Everything in my room had to be displayed like a showroom.

Having the potential for organizational structure made this possible. I seemed to be able to excel in developing an ideal surrounding for expressing myself. If I could not speak it, I would effectively present it. It wasn't until a year or two later, when I got the bigger room.

That was when I got my father to paint the ceiling black, and the walls bright orange. Then I got a white fur bedspread, with matching drapes, and of course, black satin sheets to go with it. Man, I was in heaven! I liked being alone. This was great! I had my room, my stuff, and my thoughts. When I was by myself, I felt no pressure at all. Freedom from religion, parents, peer pressure at school, lack of friends, seemed to vanish. Being alone, I felt special, for some reason. It relaxed me, and I was able to manage and develop my own maturity.

As some time past, I began to mature at a swift pace. My body was starting to change into a young woman at a very early age. I will never forget my first "special time of the month," I thought I was bleeding to death.

Still, to this day, I am waiting for "the birds and the bees talk." Clearly, it is way too late as the time has passed that I can no longer bear children. As my body began to mature exceedingly rapidly, my self-esteem was also changing.

My self-awareness was starting to be established. The frequent outbreaks of anger, uncontrollable crying, and outbursts of uncontrolled laughter drove my mother crazy. Unfortunately, I seemed to get pleasure from it continuously. At this time, I was at least getting the attention that I wanted, or maybe I was spending too much time in my room.

However, the case may be, it gave me increased enjoyment to be the center of attention.

PEER PRESSURE

At school, it was not as fun. My parents encouraged and promoted my educational performance. I will say that they went up and beyond in that area of child-rearing. They tried to establish the best possible education for me. The resources were always there for quality learning. My dad used to tell me. "You can do anything you set your mind to. It depends on how bad you want it." However, my overwhelming desire for acceptance, and to fit in, was starting to somewhat disagree with these standards of thinking.

But it seemed that no matter how hard I tried; I still could not connect with my peers. So, being the analytical creature that I was, a plan of action had to make.

Back in the mid-'70s, effectively controlling the students was a reasonably easy task. Children were always well monitored. In junior high, the worst situation that happened was a kid brought a switchblade to school. The knife was retrieved, and the student escorted out of the building. From my understanding, he was expelled from the public-school system. Nowadays, school facilities have metal detectors for gun control. Teachers and school administrators should be paid more than professional athletes. That is just my opinion.

Having the much-needed desire to be like everyone else, I proceeded with my plans. The first solution was to look like my peers. So, I asked my mother to take me shopping for a new wardrobe. Wanting to look older was my primary target. So, therefore, I had to buy outfits that enhanced my girlish figure. Mom and Dad didn't seem to approve too much of my choice of garments. Of course, acquiring the right jewelry to match was a must. Wearing make-up seemed to be effective also. Max Factor was the most popular selling product at that time. Mother was absolutely against this and refused to buy it. So, I figured that if she would not provide it for me, then there would have to be a way to get it myself. There were not enough funds with my allowance; therefore, I just swiped it from places that we shopped at. Department store security back in the '70s consisted of hired security personnel. The concept of computerized monitors had not been developed yet. We had not evolved in technology that far at this time. So no, I never had a PC growing up, or a cell phone. By taking something that did not belong to me, also put me in good standing with my peers. After all, everyone my age was doing so. The electric rush that I got, by doing something I wasn't supposed to be doing, was well worth the risk of getting caught. Actually, to my belief now, this action was impulsive behavior. However, at this time, I wanted to do what I had to because wanting to interact effectively with my peers was very important to me. I wanted to belong.

So, there I was. I believed that if I changed my attire, to influence others into thinking that I was as cool as them, I was in. Well, that was a mistake. What I was trying to do was to convey a positive personal image. It seems as if it had the opposite effect. I truly believed that if I changed my image to fit the standards of other people's lives that I would fit in. The feeling of acceptance almost engulfed my thought control. The impact of stress that I was feeling was making it impossible to concentrate on my schoolwork. Therefore, my perfect grades declined dramatically. My A's went to C's, then D's, and finally starting to fail quite a few subjects. This caused a lot of friction at home.

The atmosphere at home was starting to suffer, as well. I was always being compared with my brother and his educational accomplishments. Every night at dinner, I had to listen to my parents criticize my efforts. All of my mistakes and shortcomings were aired right there. The respect and opinions that I even remotely cared about at this time in my life were my friends. That is all any teenager cares about. So, with that in mind, I would dismiss myself from the table, not in a pleasant way, go to my room, and slam the door. This continuous course of action would quickly gain the attention of my parents.

My strategy had worked. I got the attention that I needed. When I got into my room, I cranked up the music to make them feel even worse. But when I got alone and sulked for a while, the realization hit me, that I don't seem to be able to fit in anywhere. Something different about me made it difficult to interact and build positive relationships with people. Conveying a positive personal image seemed hopeless and impossible. I had no idea what was wrong with me. I could not focus on my studies, the inability to finish any given task at school and home. I was repetitious with everything that I did, and all of my actions had to be done with repetitious order. So why couldn't I concentrate at school? Why couldn't I display a calm temperament with my parents?

The more I thought, the more confused I became. So, I stayed to myself. There was one question that started to pop into my thoughts when I was alone.

Where's God?

THE TEENAGE RUNAWAY

The time spent in reform schools and being analyzed continuously by shrinks was ineffective. My parents had given up on trying to reform me. Looking back, I don't blame them. It wasn't until later in life that I understood the responsibility of parenting when I had my children. As we all do.

Since I was allowed to seek my personal growth and development, I took advantage of the opportunity. Hanging out at the shopping center with friends and smoking weed, became my new way of life. This sure beat the isolation that I felt when I was at home. At home, and even in my room, there was a consistent feeling of isolation. Partying sure was fun. Then one day, I was handed a bottle of TJ Swan. I will never forget that day! My eyes were opened. It was the first day I ever got drunk. My whole life had meaning. Never, since childhood, had ever felt more comfortable in my surroundings. This was the first of many drinking binges. When I drank, "all" of my imperfections vanished, I found God again. There he was, in that bottle of wine. I was complete with all of the knowledge I ever needed.

As I was getting into my "newfound religion"; nothing else seemed to matter to me. There was freedom from sorrow, guilt, and pain. My parents' opinions did not matter anymore. My education was the least of my worries. I háde real friends now, mostly boys because they had the money to buy me booze. Partying and staying up all night was my daily routine. Sometimes I would be gone for days on end. One time I was brutally raped at gunpoint by five men when hitchhiking. I stopped after that. This was before I had hitchhiked all around the southern states. In these times, it was cool to do so. Ted Bundy messed that up.

When my parents tried to develop new strategies to pull me back to their world, I rebelled even more. When I partied, all of my insecurities were gone. No way was anyone going to take that away from me. Not this time. My self-esteem had come back, and I was in control this time. I was a decent, loving, and caring individual, and people like me. This was what I had been looking for all of my life. Unfortunately, these feelings of contentment were only achieved when I was buzzed or intoxicated. That is where I got the nickname "Buzzy." Anyhow, I liked myself now.

The more I drank, the security within me was heightened.

My life was meaningful and had a purpose. Life started to revolve around me now because, after all, I was God. As time went by, my mom and dad showed deep concern for wellbeing. Despite my actions, my mother remained silent for the most part. Except for the tears rolling down her cheeks. Remembering this time of my life, to this day, even as I am writing this now, hurts me so badly. It brings such remorse to me. The past has to be let go; however, this image of her seems to have had a profound impact on me. Because, as an adult now, hurting another human being is unacceptable to me. You must always respect and keep a close rapport with your family. Keep in mind that this is of the utmost importance in life.

My inappropriate behavior at home would soon find me in the hands of the authorities regularly. The police would find me, bring me home, and as soon as they left, I would be right back out the window. It was a conspiracy against me to ruin and take back control of my life. They hated me, and probably wish that I had never been born. I was starting to analyze my existence. One time I stole my mom's Ford Pinto, with some acquaintances, and drove it down to Tennessee. Since my father taught me how to drive a tractor at an early, this was not a problem.

A person would have thought I had been driving for years. But his coaching and training skills with farming did not include this.

Well, after that escapade, my parents came down and retrieved the car.

I was left in the county jail for three weeks, then flown back to Maryland, in shackles, and put back in the detention center. I just couldn't get a break here. I remained in reform and institutions after that, until I was around 15. When I finally came back home, I made a promise to my parents that I would overcome my weaknesses and do right by them. I made a conscious decision to establish goals and to work cooperatively with my parents. My motives were genuine. Besides, what my parents didn't know wouldn't hurt them.

THE PROSTITUTE

Gradually, I started experimenting with other drugs. This time of my life, I really cannot recall a lot of memories, because I was too stoned to remember. Wanting to be accepted by others, I engaged in the use of PCP, LSD, Hash, Cocaine, Speed, Uppers, Downers, and Marijuana. Even with all these chemicals in my system, alcohol was my favorite. Somehow along the way, I was introduced to heroin. Now that was a dangerous "twilight zone" trip.

I was hooked the first time I ever shot it up. That lasted a few months. Thanks to a good friend that helped me recognize, I was making a grave mistake.

I could write a whole novel alone about this timeframe of my life; however, it would be unwise to elaborate on stories because there is too much to tell. My frequent drug use left me not knowing where I was or who I was with most of the time. But somehow, I was able to meet a nice young man. I was 16 when I met my friend. He was seven years older than me, making him 23, or he said he was at least. He once stated he had two birth certificates.

I'm going to let that one go.

Somehow, the content of his birth certificates did not matter to me. He was active at purchasing beer and could get me out of that terrible house. Recognizing that I had the opportunity to leave, I packed my bags and prepared myself for the opportunity of a lifetime. I was happy.

I was so in love with this man; I could not believe that I was so lucky to have found true happiness again with another person. This time was going to be different.

With a strong sense of well-being and trust towards another, I began my journey. My life was going to be devoted to taking care of this man. He loved and adored me so much. He was a man; it was his responsibility to take care of me. After all, my parents did not delegate responsibility successfully. My past conflicts in life were the lack of their poor parenting skills. That was my opinion at the time. The fact that God did not want anything to do with me anymore made it clear I was alone. I was accepted by my boyfriend Brian, just the way I was, I did not need to change.

That was all I needed, and I felt wanted again. So, we started to make plans for the future.

THE FIRST MARRIAGE

Brian and I moved in with his parents. After a few months, he proposed marriage to me. After making so many unpractical decisions in my life, saying yes was the best option. This person cared deeply for me, and I could not let him down. My parents' critical response was typical, as always. However, knowing how determined and self-directed I was, they knew they had no other alternative but to be supportive. I had the self-confidence that it would be mature stability for me, so we proceeded to make plans.

My relationship with my parents was starting to build a climate of trust again. The time spent away from them was probably the critical factor. At 16, I was displaying a very high level of maturity. I was starting to understand their motives for behavior. If felt more grown-up than ever. As a few months went by, there were personality changes with Brian. When he drank, he became verbally abusive. His verbal expressions turned into violent fits of rage. He was always sorry after the fact, and cried like a baby, and to forgive him. I always did. He had promised that it would never happen again. I believed him because he loved me so much.

Besides, he was a very nice person when he wasn't intoxicated. Of course, I never told my parents of his outbreaks, in fear, especially with my dad, he might have eliminated him off this planet. One time, he wanted to close the cement lid on him when he was in our well checking the water level. Who knows how he would have handled this situation. My father had a sense of humor I will say that.

Brian and I were unpractical with our money, what little we did have. Therefore, he made me sleep with his friends for money. He was unproductive with making money himself, so I guess he turned the job over to me. We would make our way to the local strip clubs, and he would pimp me out there.

My commitment and eagerness to please him made this acceptable. I carefully followed his directions and complied. After all, he loved me. There were times when his 70-year-old stepfather partook in the arranged meetings.

When we obtained our own apartment, it was my understanding that life was going to get better. I did not party as much at this time of my life; Brian had enough for both of this.

He had a way of continually producing more friction than I had anticipated. His drunken rages continued for days on end. Drinks and food were slammed in my face daily.

I was yelled at and humiliated in public by him. That is "when" I was allowed to go out. When we walked together around other people, I had to walk behind him, and I was not allowed to look at anyone in the eyes. That just was not permitted. If I did, I would get my face bashed in when we got home.

It was at this time I became pregnant with Brian's baby. The difficult decision to have an abortion was made. I was not willing to accept the responsibility and decided to terminate the pregnancy.

My mother went with me. We went to an abortion clinic, and the procedure was done. The pain was tormenting. Throughout my life, I didn't think too much of it. It was not until recently that I understood what I had done. I do not take a moral standing with this controversial issue. However, personally, for me, I believe there should have been more options to explore.

I decided to have sex; therefore, it was my responsibility to use protection. For me, this situation, I believe in my heart now, that I murdered my child. Again, this is only my perception of the situation at hand.

There is no judgment towards myself because I was unaware of the choices I had at this time. This was a decision that I made at a very young age.

I hold full accountability for my actions. This is in the past.

After the abortion, I married Brian. I loved him so much. It was a beautiful wedding. Yes, I wore white. My life seemed to be full of so many disappointments so far. Maybe this would work out for the best. He wasn't hitting me as much, so maybe he learned his lesson.

I tried to show him as much attention as possible, so maybe I could tolerate a few beatings a week. He really didn't mean to hurt me the day after the clinical procedure anyway.

Brian used to sleepwalk. We lived in a three-story apartment building in northern Virginia.

He walked over near the window, I swear, I almost pushed him out. His parents knew of his sleeping habits, so I could have gotten away with it. I deliberately threw in some humor there.

Sometimes in life, having a sense of humor is all you need. Without having a substantial income coming in, we were forced to move. This is where I was forced to watch his vehicle run over our cat. I tolerated his behavior because he loved me, and I him. The embarrassment of going back home outweighed the importance of making a marriage work. I was a dedicated wife. I was going to solve any problems with him before they became too critical anyway.

THE LAST STRAW

We found a small three-room house, which sat beside a preacher's home.

I knew that this adjustment was going to be sound. We went to his church one night. All I can remember was the loud music, and the congregation rolling around the floor, looking as if they were having seizures. I walked right on back out the back door. As if the fire and brimstone stories of my youth didn't scare me.

This indeed did! My husband was not too happy about this. He yelled at me all the way home.

When we arrived back at the house, he had calmed down quite a lot.

Everything was hushed and peaceful. I decided to go to sleep. I needed to use the bathroom, so when I came out, there was Brian, standing in front of me with a huge butcher knife. He had a crazed look in his eyes, unlike anything I had ever seen before. Before I could blink, he starts swinging the blade at me.

At this time, I believed that he wanted to kill me. The risk of losing him had to be made quite abruptly. I fought back. We rumbled for a short period. He swung the knife; I ducked and took my fists and knocked the holy wind out of him.

He kicked me in the stomach several times. At that time, I ran out to the preachers' home. At least this time, there was no confusion in his mind that was the last time he would ever lay his hands on me.

The pastor opened the door, so I could make a phone call to my dad.

I told him what had been happening and pleaded with him to come get me. The situation was well handled. He did.

I thought, knowing my father's overprotection of me, he was going to bring a shotgun. The pastor denied that anything ever happened, even though there was blood running down my cheek, and an imprinted fist mark on my face. I guess God wasn't here either.

We went home. I never spoke to Brian again, until he was forced to sign the divorce papers. It was done in a public restaurant. The encounter was brief. This time, my eyes looked straight ahead.

THE BABY

It was such a relief to be home. I had made the right decision. Before retiring for the night, my parents were assured that my self-improvement goals would be met. This time their practical advice would be significantly considered. Collapsing in the bathroom from sheer exhaustion, my brother and Dad place me into my "own" bed. I slept soundly for a brief period.

I awoke in the middle of the night, with the most case of abdominal cramps that any woman could have during a menstrual cycle. It seemed as if I just got my period. This continued for several days. During the day, it wasn't so bad, but it was unbearable for me to sleep at night. The number of blood clots was extremely abnormal. One morning, after the pain had ceased to a tolerable level, I went to use the bathroom. I felt a large mass of a blot clot near my vagina. As I pulled it away, strings of mucus were still hanging on. It wouldn't tear away, as I tried with maximum effort, I realized what it was. These were two little feet that I was tugging on. Trying to grasp the concept of being pregnant was difficult, let alone what was happening. My dad rushed me to the clinic.

The baby dropped from my uterus into my underwear.

The doctor put the fetus on the table, and I begged to see him. It was a little boy. I was around five months pregnant. He was fully formed but extremely small. I was in shock. Later in my child producing days, I had several more miscarriages. We went to the hospital, where a D&C was performed.

This experience had a profound impact on me.

Dad was not too pleased, because he yelled at me the whole time during the trip to the hospital. This didn't make the situation any better. Now, I believe he was just as traumatized as me.

His anger was his way of dealing with the situation at hand. He sometimes had a problem with displaying positive responses to adverse situations.

I believe he was just overworked.

It was just his way of showing me that he loved me.

It was at this time of my life that awareness of my strength came into perspective. My display of positive, confident, and calm attitude towards my parents was beginning to bring harmony back in my life. Wanting my parents' approval once again, I decided to go back to school.

My good intentions were strong but not practical. It was almost impossible to relate to anyone there. Since I was in the 8th grade, married, and had been out there in "the real world," I could not communicate effectively. This made it hard to find real friends. My acceptance from my peers was declined; therefore, that lasted a few months. It didn't matter because; I was having a tough time holding my head up in class anyway.

With moderation, I had started back partying again.

A NEW START

Between the ages of seventeen to eighteen, I excelled in my humorous wit. My two best friends and I mastered the art of playing jokes and pranks. One time, my friend Dolly and I called a number from random that we retrieved from the phone book. We asked the woman by name if her husband was there. Of course, by the first name also. She confusingly said, "No." The lady asked what it was about. I told her, "just tell him I had a wonderful time, and to call me later."

Hours later, we called back and asked for him again. This time he was there. She gave him the phone, and he was so confused. We could hear his wife yelling at him in the background. We had to hang up, we were laughing so hard, and we almost lost our bodily functions. This was before Caller ID.

My best friend Peter and I hung out a lot. He drove and was twenty-one. It was a platonic relationship. We were buddies and partners in crime. He taught me how to shoot people in the buttocks as they were leaning over to get their mail. Look, it was a bb gun and only pumped up a few times. It only felt like a slight bee sting. It seemed harmless at the time, now I know better. Dad had taught me how to use a shotgun at an early age, so I had a pretty accurate aim.

There was one time when Peter, Dolly, and a few other friends, took some old clothes and stuffed them with newspaper. We put a wig on the top of the shoulders and laid it in the road. We placed it strategically in the middle to make it look like a real person.

With a knife in the chest and simulated blood, we used ketchup, which looked authentic. We proceeded to hide in the isolated, wooded area around the house.

We wanted a clear view of this spectacular event that was about to take place. It was dark, and it was raining profoundly. We waited. To my surprise, two cars came, and ran right over it and kept ongoing. Along came the third. Run over again. We were starting to become disappointed. Lo, and behold, they screeched their tires. They stopped. Within a few seconds, they proceeded in reverse. They ran back over it again. We could not believe it. Being the only car in sight, it was reasonably easy to see what was going on. We heard some people get out of the car, and I woman screamed, "Oh my God, we killed somebody"! There was hollering and screaming, and then silence. A man loudly said, "Hey, this thing isn't real"!

They wanted to find us. We all scattered and ran like crazy. Our adrenaline made us like track athletics.

When we all got back to the house, my mom had just gotten home from work. Given the fact we were clearly out of breath and had the look of guilt on our face. She asked if we were out getting stoned. We denied it, not wanting to tell her what happened. We were. An individual would have to be under the influence of alcohol or narcotics to pull a stunt like that. Later in life, I realized how dangerous it was doing that. Nobody was hurt; therefore, I don't care who you are.

That's funny! Besides, we never did it again after that. Although there were many times before, we had.

CAREFREE PARTY DAYS

It was at my friend's house, Peter, that I had my 18th birthday party. His house was packed. I would like to say I had an excellent time, but I can't recall. The beginning of this event was exceptional. Crawling on the floor from a hangover was the next thing I remember. That was because I could not stand. Everyone said I had a blast, so I took their word for it. The hangover lasted for days.

Well, here it was. I was of legal age and ready to take on the world. The past was fading, and I had valuable insights and a flow of fresh ideas for my future. In 1981, the drinking age was eighteen. However, I was going to bars since the age of 14; it was not that special. They did not ask for ID back then. If you looked 18 and conducted yourself maturely, they did not care. But, I had never been to a real nightclub legally. This was different. My true love had been found again, and I could be myself. Drinking gave me a sense of security that I had not felt since my childhood. When I drank, I was able to express my views clearly, and speak in a positive tone.

In the clubs, when interacting with people, I displayed a relaxed and pleasant demeanor. I found God.

Going out and hanging with my new friends was fantastic. My nightly club habits were starting to become expensive, so I decided to look for employment eagerly. My first job was working at McDonald's. We were overworked and underpaid. It did not matter, because it allowed me the funds to go out. That did not last too long; working was crippling my other priorities. Having fun and getting favorable attention from strangers was the plan. I continued to seek attention and respect from people. Other individuals' opinions mattered to me still at this time. Always striving for perfection, this was important to me. I wanted to conform to others standards of living. My values didn't matter, because I just wanted to be accepted by others.

Two favorite spots found my appeal. It was in this time that Michael Jackson's "Thriller" album was released. Madonna made her first debut, and "Flashlight," by Parliament, was playing over the sound system in the clubs. This timeframe was the end of the disco days. "Saturday Night Fever" was becoming a classic. But, "Saturday Night Live," was giving our teens dynamic and enlightening entertainment.

GI JANE

A few months rolled by, and the music industry's accelerating changing conditions were starting to bore me. Eagerly wanting to assume higher responsibly in my life, I decided to join the Army. My parents strongly encouraged this idea. Finally, I was living up to their expectations. The fact is, I had already enlisted before I told them. They were happy.

The atmosphere surrounded by military training was gratifying. It was tough at times. But here, I gained self-confidence, grasp new routines, and learn strong self-control.

This is where I also learned how to drink beer from a straw. I had built within myself, a strong sense of teamwork and proper codes of conduct.

The consistent logical thinking was something that I lacked. It was at this time that I was capable of understanding practical concepts.

Positive reinforcement was what I needed. We will forget about the sergeants' light bulb eating habits. This was done for entertainment purposes only. So, when I finally came home, the Army's behavior modification gave me a sense of purpose. My parents were pleased. It seemed as if my past failures had been erased. Things were about to get better. Maybe God is around.

It was at this time in my life that I was starting to develop a keen sense of responsibility. I achieved an expert badge with an M-16 rifle, as well as accuracy with an M-60 machine gun. With the hand grenade training, it was the lower badge. That was only because I feared them. I did blow up a tank in the field, however. But the vehicle was "not" the target. Live grenades, in my hand, count to seven; yeah, right! I just had to achieve bottom-line results.

With my new understanding of personal confidence, I was ready to take on the world. I was able to communicate with my parents. Responsibility around the house was becoming favorable to my Mom. She worked many hours at this time. She was a real-go-getter. So was my dad; my mother would go to work, and he would "go get her."

At least that is what his hat said.

When I went out to clubs and did that quite a lot, I was able to interact better with strangers. My intellectual level had also started to develop.

I was starting to believe in myself once again.

THE 2ND MARRIAGE

My friend and I went to our local club, as we did every weekend.

I met a guy. We seemed to hit it off. To even my surprise, I gave him my real phone number. This was an act that wasn't in my character.

Mostly, I just wanted drinks and no conversation. We dated for a few weeks and became deeply in love with each other. I was indeed in love this time. But it might have been the fact he always had weed. So, did his friends. One gentleman had a room of weed at his house that would have put: "Cheech and Chong" to shame! This was when I was introduced to crack. Wow, what a rush. This was in the time era where one would freebase. This expensive habit was too much for my taste. So, I just had my beer and left all that fun to Jake. He didn't like to drink too much anyway.

Jake proposed to me, I, of course, accepted. This was not an excuse to leave the premises of my parents' home.

Our happiness together was the only thing that mattered to me. We had wedding plans for June, but an unforeseen pregnancy made us change it to December. This was a baby conceived from love and was very much wanted. Even though sometimes, when I get mad, I tell the kid they were conceived at a local drive-in. Just joking with them, knowing it "was" the truth, however. This unexpected pregnancy was by no means the reason we got married.

I want to make that especially clear.

We just had to move up the date a little. I do not encourage pre-marital sex, nor do I condone the act. My viewpoint now is a nonjudgmental one.

We had a small but quaint wedding. This time I wore a long purple gown with matching veil. My friend Dolly and Peter were among the guests there.   Peter walked me down the aisle. My father refused to cooperate with this function.   It wasn't until later that I came to reasoning with his actions.

Looking back, maybe Dolly should have escorted Peter and me down the aisle. Or mom; could have walked Dolly and I. Anyhow, it was a beautiful wedding. It went beyond what was expected for a second wedding. I was with Jake, and we were expecting our first child. That was all that mattered. I was happy and was starting to think of God for the first time in a while.

Jake and I purchased a new 1983 Windsor mobile home. My idea of these homes was extremely misguided. It was large. It had three bedrooms, two baths, a huge kitchen, a living room with a fireplace, and ours. My first real home had been acquired. We were together, and we were happy.

MY FIRSTBORN

As the months rolled by, I got enormously huge. Being pregnant, I took advantage of consuming anything that didn't walk. That was apparent since I could not see my feet anymore.

It was an agonizing summer. But the day had arrived. It was in the hospital that I realized the meaning of "the everlasting burning pits of hell," as my pastor of youth put it. My second response was to locate my mother and kiss her feet. Thirdly, it was to take Jake, standing in front of me, and make sure he could never produce children again. You remember Leonna Bobbitt, right? The military taught me innovative strategies. Rationalization during these hours was not possible.

We went to the delivery room. One hour later, she was born. As they gently placed her on my chest, I looked into her wide-open eyes, with tears rolling down my cheeks. I said, 'I knew it was you all along". I closed my eyes and found God. I had my reason for living.

My life was perfect now. Jake demonstrated the ability to provide a quality of life for his family that was acceptable to me. He conveyed his sincere appreciation for me and was a wonderful father. This was the happiest time of my life. It remains in my heart. My father used to say that; "family was the most important thing in the world." I will say it took me a long time to see that.

MY SECOND BORN

Two years went by, and I was pregnant with our second child. We were hoping that the baby would be a boy this time. I had learned from my previous delivery to make sure the epidural was asked well in advance. This was an effortless delivery. The pain was reduced to a minimum; Actually, I was so numb that I couldn't even push.

They had to take the baby with forceps.

When the child popped out, I yelled, not being able to see, "what is it? What is it"? "It's a boy," the nurse yelled across the room. I believe Peter cried, as much as I did. We were now complete. We had a son and a daughter. The nurse had my son in an incubator for a while, because he showed signs of jaundice. Upon looking at him, I told the doctor to put him back in; he wasn't done yet. That was a joke.

So here we were, confronted with the responsibility of raising a family. I was 22, a proud mother of two, and I was the happiest person that I had ever been in my entire life. Nothing else mattered to me except my family. I was successfully demonstrating the ability to be a good role model for my children. My relationship with my parents took on a whole new meaning. I believe this was the first time I had ever heard them use the word "proud." Looking back, it was not. My perception of them, as a child, was slightly altered. I was a kid, what did I know anyway? I was drug-free, except for a few drinks here and there. The desire to party had diminished. My time was dedicated to the care and well-being of my family.

As a few years went by, I was happy. I was able to face problems with confidence and assurance. I tried to follow in my mom's footsteps by trying to display the strong, dynamic leadership that my mother had.

Memories of her warm and caring ways had a profound impact on my mothering techniques. My determination to be a "normal" person was much desired then. I still seemed to possess the character trait of acceptance and belonging. So, I started to conform my clothing, hairstyle, and makeup techniques. I believed that this would bring a positive image of me to everyone, especially my family. My decision to stay at home was much desired. The option back in the early and mid-'80s was favorable, as well as economically feasible. This decision was the most rewarding experience of my life. I have the utmost respect for any individual who accepts the responsibility of the growth and development of another human being.

SUZIE HOMEMAKER

It was then that I became so consumed with being a good parent that I strived for complete perfection. As Jake worked all the time, I remained at home, delegating responsibility there. I did not work. As an Army Reservist, my duties only called for me to be there one weekend a month.

That was exciting for me because sometimes the kids got on my nerves. You must know I was there for them 24/7. We never went out to social gatherings. That was a thing in the past. There was one summer that I sold Avon and Tupperware. That made Peter upset because I was my own best customer.

As a couple of years went by, our life was practical and secure. I had finally become the "perfect" daughter that my parents had always wanted. I was happy. I had God.

By the time my children were 1 and 3 years old, opportunities for a new life sounded exciting. Back in the mid-'80s, all my childhood girlfriends had been working outside the home. The feeling of boredom and isolation began to overcome me once again. All of the neighborhood moms would leave their children with me since I was home all the time. I was also known as; "the cupcake lady." The provisions for treats were always made. They must have assumed that the time and energy I had for their kids was my only sense of purpose. Maybe they were right. But I had made a personal commitment to pleasing others. Besides, I was happy.

Every night, dinner was always served on the table when Jake came home.

The house was clean, orderly, and creatively decorated. I was a loyal wife and an exceptional mother.

HIDDEN SECRETS

Well, this structured atmosphere got old, real fast. The feelings of boredom and the repetitiveness of daily life were starting to give me feelings of resentment again. Here I was all alone, giving my life to others and seemingly not getting anything in return. I was starting to feel insignificant and useless as a human being.

Everything appeared to be going well.

Surrounded by love and the family I always wanted; I was still lonely. Something was missing. I wanted my life, friends, and, most of all, my freedom back. All these years, I had become what others had expected of me. My life was centered on everyone. So with that in mind, I decided to take a trip to the store, the liquor store.

This was when I started to pay more attention to my own happiness than my family's needs. I began drinking again, a little earlier in the evening each day. It didn't present a problem for Jake, because he was smoking his weed. My parents didn't know, so that was cool. My parental responsibly was well maintained; therefore, I knew that my behavior was acceptable. Besides, when I drank, I had energy and vitality to perform my daily tasks. This worked quite effectively for several years.

As my daily responsibilities became less important to me, I had acquired the close friendship of a neighbor. We were drinking buddies. She introduced me to whiskey drinking. My new friend made it possible to get out of the house quite frequently; she lived within walking distance. I would either take the kids, or I waited until Jake got home. I left "him" the responsibility of watching them.

My display of affection towards Jake and my children needed improvement at this time. They just did not seem to understand me. I found it challenging to explain to my husband the need for self-purpose. When he criticizes my actions or behavior, I was very articulate in telling him, "where to go." He gave up after a while and let me proceed with my plans. So, for the next few years, I enjoyed myself. God was finally allowing me to be happy.

The day had finally arrived when my daughter started kindergarten.

Since this was our first separation from each other, I passed by the school numerous times that morning.

In tears, I had flashbacks of "Barney and Mister Rodgers." These were her favorite TV shows at the time. This era was when Beta and VHS tapes were popular. We did not have cable back then. Playing Atari video games at home was the new pass time for kids.

My son was given much favorable attention at this time. Being that now, it was just him and I. It was at this time, I was developing a strong bond with my youngest child. Assuming that since most of my friends were always guys, this did not surprise me.

You could not keep me away from that kid. As much as a high degree of recognition was given to both of my children, my son and I were building an extremely close rapport. He was my little man. I had two miscarriages between the two, so this successful effort was accomplished.

My daughter displayed self-reliance and independence at an early age.

Her first words were,' I do it myself".

Thirty-some years later, she still maintains that personal empowerment. She had truly learned to accomplish a positive direction in life successfully. This will be shared at a later time. I am so proud of her. However, it was clearly defined at home, who defined responsibility and authority. Even though she was capable of a wide range of decision making, I kept a tight rein on her.

When my son started school, I had my freedom back. I was consistently involved with their education.

Back then, child abduction was gaining a lot of attention in the media. I closely monitored them at all times. Even when I went to my friends' house to drink, they had to come with me. They had other kids to play with; therefore, I capitalized on the opportunity to maintain my own momentum. Looking back, it was a lack of common sense, and my desire to engage in self-indulgence.

THE PATHWAY TO DESTRUCTION

As a season passed, the burden of having the children always by my side was harboring my inability to have freedom. Still seeking the acceptance of others, I tried to juggle my drinking habit with my family image. My mother and father, as well as Jake's parents, were always giving their critical opinion about our irresponsible parenting actions. This made me mad and highly upset. So I just drank more, and he smoked his weed. It was at this time he started using cocaine more frequently.

I didn't partake as much, because it cost too much, and it seemed to be a wasted high. As long as there were enough funds for my whiskey, wine coolers, and beer, I was content. Besides, if they would just back off a bit, let us run our own lives, I wouldn't have to drink as much. The reason I had to drink as much was that their interference affected my personal performance as a mom.

With this in mind, my "spiritual quest" was well sought after for harmony and peace in my life. As it states in the Bible, Matthew 7:7 "Ask and it will be given to you; seek, and ye shall find; knock, and it will be opened to you; this was an understatement. I don't think the intentions of that statement applied here. Never less, the plan of action seemed positive and realistic at the time.

I was living the life I had always wanted. I was happy. When I drank all of my imperfections went away. As also did my recollection of certain events did too. In the morning, at the school bus stop, I had my coffee cup filled with my favorite beer, and my purse ready at hand with refills.

Having a crafty art of illusion, I periodically blew on the top, so it appeared to be coffee. I still wanted everyone to have a positive image of me.

Running out of beer was thinkable to me.

Jake didn't have time for me because he was doing his "own thing." That was fine with me; it gave me more time to be alone anyway. I liked being alone. The time had come again, where I was finally becoming my own person. The importance of "my" key role in life was much desired. My family didn't matter, because "I" was finally in charge. Nothing would stand in my way this time. My life was finally under control.

THE JOB LAY OFF

Shortly after that, my drinking habit became a daily desire.

The only problem that I had with it was when Jake had insufficient funds to buy it. At this time, his job was laying off workers. He was the next in line. That situation didn't help at all. I started to neglect my children's welfare, as well as my dedication and loyalty to my husband. We could no longer communicate effectively with each other. All conversations would always end up in an argument. So our closeness and the reliability we once had on each other for support was spiraling downwards.

With Jake's new unemployment status, love for his drug habits, and my booze, it made a dysfunctional surrounding for the children.

Our verbal arguments had become more frequent as time went by. One Christmas, I had turned the tree upside down, and the decorations went everywhere, as well as destroying many personal items of his. I tried to develop a resourceful solution to our problems. It was apparent that our children were developing emotional issues.

Realizing their personal growth and development was at risk, we decided to change.

THE CHURCH LADY

We started going to church regularly and became members quite quickly. The children attended Sunday school, as well. We had identified our weaknesses and wanted to change.

I, of course, had to modify my appearance altogether again. Now, I was playing the church lady role. The need for self-improvement made my parents pleased. I was happy.

The changed atmosphere didn't affect my drinking habits as much. I could not interact and communicate with social grace unless I had a few six-packs in me. Looking back, I am sure my poise and first impressions were not that attractive, as I perceived them to be because my Pastor told me that I could not go on any more church functions intoxicated.

The only explanation I wanted was, how did he know? He even confronted me about coming to church slightly buzzed all the time. Of course, it was denied. It was then that I realized that now God was even critical of me.

I just could not get a break. So, I went home and got drunk.

I had spent my whole life trying to gain respect and acceptance of others. I had to get drunk. My inability to rationalize overcame my emotions. My downward spiral of self-destruction was in motion. Going from my average weight of 125 pounds, I was starting to exceed the obese weight of 205lbs. Consumption of fatty foods was not the cause. My diet consisted mostly of beer and liquor, and the occasional 23 or 24 wine coolers I drank.

THE BLAME STARTS HERE

My attitude towards life and others was becoming one of hatred and regret. I was beginning to blame Jake for our ongoing problems. I blamed my son and daughter for my drinking because it was their fault I was stuck in this situation. But most of all, I blamed my parents for giving me life. Since God finally decided to show up and disregard me, too, I proceeded to do as I pleased. I can not elaborate on all of the events that took place, because I don't have enough time to do so.

I had not seen my childhood friend for quite some time, as she also had her life and a family. Dolly stopped by the house one day. With her deepest sincerity, she expressed her concerns for me. She had this insane idea that I might have a small problem with drinking. How could "I" have a drinking problem; I defensively told her. First of all, I wanted to clarify to her that my responsible drinking did not affect anyone. Secondly, I was a wife and a mother, was living in a beautiful home, and had a strong interpersonal confidence. And thirdly, why the hell, was she still standing in front of me? I told her to leave, and she reluctantly did.

Great, now the whole world was indeed against me. So, I got drunk.

Reflecting now, the house was starting to show signs of neglect.

The children's attitudes were changing, and my relationship with my husband was becoming distant. I did consider the message she was trying to relay to me.

I thought to myself; alcoholics were dirty, homeless, and men. They didn't want responsibility, so they lived in the street. No problem, with my analogy of what was said from Dolly, is that she had lost her mind. The comment hurt me deeply, so I terminated our friendship. Not knowing at the time, she only had my best interest at heart and was trying to be a friend.

THE CAT AND THE FBI

Brian had been laid off for numerous months. Our economic stability was threatened. The food stamps we received were not of significant value to feed a growing family. I believe he was selling them for drugs. Back in the '80s, they were of paper form. I sold a few to get some beer. We had bought a new 1984 Chevy Caviler some time back. The car got repossessed twice. The 3rd time we just let it go. A few years earlier, the neighbors' cat had repeatedly jumped up and scratched the entire hood. Being the sole creator of originality, I decided to teach it a lesson one day.

For months I watched for the time frame when the cat was placed outside. The hours were consistent, ok, no problem. Now, I had to get the cat. I knew the path the animal was going to take, so I waited patiently around the side of the shed. Finally, I pounced on it, held its little paws, applied super-glue, and stuck the bastard to the side of their house. This was my way of getting back. When the police and fire department came, I was nowhere in sight.

Later, in life, I became a member of the United States Humane Society and a dog breeder. I had such remorse for this act of unkindness towards an animal that I took years to get over it. Another unforgettable event that took place was when I made a bomb threat to the telephone company. The initiative was taken to use the house phone, what can I say I was drunk. We will not go into detail about the unforeseen consequences that took place. However, I will say that hour later, when four black FBI cars showed up at my door, the feeling of intoxication had gone. Fourteen hundred dollars later for an attorney, and the pure humiliation of being arrested, taught me a valuable lesson. I shouldn't have used my phone. I should have remained friends with Dolly and used hers. That was a joke.

It was during these times when I was starting to have periods of black-outs and hallucinations. There was an image of an old grey-haired man that kept appearing on my bedroom door. Sometimes, he moved to look directly at me, but he never spoke. He only appeared when I was drinking and alone. I believed at the time it was God. One morning, one of the strangest occurrences happened to me. It was Thanksgiving morning, to be exact. After a night of exhausting arguments with my husband, I was in complete remorse of my actions. As we sat there on the bed, I cried and told him how sorry I was for everything that was said. After a few minutes of reconciliation, I happened to glance up at the closet door, which was opened. There was a strange, small, round, green ball of light rotating around me. I slowly, with great amazement, stretched out my arm and opened my hand. It descended downward in a slow-motion manner and melted in my hand. I was sober. Jake witnessed this miraculous event, so I knew that I wasn't having an acid flashback.

The bongs, pipes, and papers were gathered together and thrown in the trashcan. I quit drinking for three days. I was so proud of myself. We never again spoke of the incident.

THERE GOES OUR HOME

The week after we received a letter in the mail, it stated that the bank was foreclosing on our home. The concept of foreclosure isn't that unusual. But in this case, I have to ask, "how many of you have watched your home, and belongings get rolled off on wheels, and watch it go down the highway"?

Now I find it somewhat humorous, at the time it wasn't.

My parents were gracious enough to allow us to reside with them for a brief period until we could get on our feet again. We tried very hard to work effectively with each other.

This was hard. Having two households in a family is always challenging to deal with. Jake was still not working; however, he managed to find periodic employment. That winter, he had a temporary job as Santa Claus. The climate of trust issues had started to develop with my parents. Because, here again, they were trying to involve themselves with our life too much, and we had to sneak around to party. Our parenting skills and inappropriate behavior as parents were unsuitable to them. So we decided to move.

My father had given us an old station wagon, as we had the other car taken from us. The children, having to move again, were starting to show signs of distrust with Jake and me. This deeply disturbed me, but there was nothing I could do. So I drank. The only social outlet that we had was church. But that was starting to bore me. Of course, that perception might not have been accurate. Because at this time, my vision was blurred and vision-impaired when I was there. We had to sit in the front pews because I had to "always" be the center of attention.

They were all there for me, anyway.

The question was, where the hell was God?

POVERTY STARTS

We found a house that was affordable and suitable for the children.

They were starting to grow up fast.

Jake was still unemployed, and his temp jobs were not sufficient enough for my standards of living. The little funds that we did have were used for our alcohol and drug habits. My parents would always provide food and clothing for the children, as they always did.

We belonged to a local church.

The pastor was a member of our previous one. He had a worthy goal of obtaining his own religious establishment. It was small in membership, but his teachings were quite impressive. I am assuming that they were because I was intoxicated most of the time. He didn't judge, so we remained members. Besides, my spiritual level was heightened when I drank.

As our finances starting to decline to almost nothing, my attitude towards my kids, husband, parents, suffered as well. DMV confiscated the tags on the car we had. Jake developed a resourceful solution and created fake cardboard tags. This worked for a brief period, until "I" got pulled over. His actions, later in my life, cost me $750 before I could obtain tags for another vehicle.

Since we did not have a lot of money in those days, our limited funds of $12.00 were all I had for that Christmas. We went into the woods and chopped down a 12-foot pine tree and placed it in the living room. It was indeed a "Charlie Brown Christmas" that year. I, with my creative strategies, went to each of the children's bedroom, looked for all the toys that were not played with, and wrapped them up. I placed the gifts under the tree. By now, all 24 branches of dry, brittle pine needles had fallen to the floor. That Christmas was most memorable.

Another time I recall was that of; we will call "the pool incident."

We assembled our 12ft by 36-inch steel pool in the back yard. The responsibility to fill it with water was given to the kids. Going inside to finish my drink, I warned them not to go near the pool, until it was full. They did so.

My 9-year-old son, at the time, was starting to shows signs of hypertension and compulsiveness. As I looked out the window, he was by the pool; both hands gripped on the sides. I yelled at him and told him to get away. He didn't know I was looking, and the reaction startled him. As I watched in dismay, the inevitable happened. There goes my son, rolling down the hill, as roughly 2000 gallons of water carried him to the bottom. We never got another pool.

My behavior to his actions was intensely irrational. He ran from me, and my daughter took refuge in her bedroom. When I finally found him hiding under his bed, I whipped his buttocks profoundly.

I picked him up and thrashed him against the wall. This was one of the many times I had physically abused my children. My intense response of anger was not appropriate.

Looking back, it was fear. The situation could have resulted in severe injuries. I was just unable to express or communicate my deep concern for his well-being.

NO WAY OUT

After that, the lack of finances, my husband's addiction, and the ongoing verbal and physical abuse towards my children, had to stop. When I drank, I got angry; when I didn't have a drink in my hand, my temper was worse. My exceptional abilities to provide a well-organized house had diminished. The broken household items and shattered glass everywhere always marked my fits of rage. I could not handle my life anymore. Being alone in my bedroom, my family liked it a lot; I had time to think.

Maybe there was something wrong with me. I just felt different.

As I sat there in my room, drink in hand, I tried to rationalize my life. Always blaming others for my shortcomings and lack of good judgment, I decided to look at myself. The feelings of guilt, shame, and unfavorable acceptance tormented me. I knew what had to happen. No longer could I accept all of the pain my family was enduring because of my inability to accept responsibility. My decision had been made. I was going to take my own life.

First, I had to make sure there was enough alcohol. Then, I had to plan a strategy that didn't acquire too much pain. After a good 12-pack and a half, I proceeded to drive down the road, towards a river.

The lack of police checkpoints made it easy. The intention of driving my car into the river was the target. A half an hour later, still driving, still drinking, gave me a lot of time to think. I knew that my family would be safe, and there would be no more tears in their eyes.

I was happy. I don't recall blacking out, but before I realized it, I had turned the car around, and I was headed home. To this day, I don't know if the thoughts of suicide brought fear, or this was a "divine interaction." Maybe it was God.

When I got home, my incompetent ability to commit suicide made me mad. Therefore, I took a whole bottle of sleeping pills. They didn't kill me, of course, but I had a hell of a conversation with the door handle.

We were in the process of having to move again, and this was our last week at "this" house. This is where things got weird. Every night I sat outside gazing at the house. Sitting there, like a zombie, I watched a light grey apparition climb up the side of the building. It appeared to be a woman. Having these visions before, she did not frighten me. Being that nobody else wanted me around, maybe she needed me. I tried to take pictures, but they would never seem to develop correctly. I brushed it off. Maybe I really was starting to lose my mind. As the eviction took place at the end of the week, we moved to central North Carolina.

POOR TO POORER

We took residence behind Jakes' grandparent's house. It was old, had four rooms, and no heat. The weather-beaten wood siding desperately needed to be painted.

It didn't matter though, because we had our own home again. His relatives were very nice, and they liked me. We all got along quite well. Jake successively gained employment. Eager to make this work, I too got a job in the hotel housekeeping industry. For the first time in a while, I was starting to feel a degree of self-worth. We were maintaining our finances, our relationship together was improving, and the kids were happy. My temperament issues were replaced with a calm and relaxed attitude.

My overindulgence with alcohol was starting to lose its desire.

This decision to move down here was the best solution to solve our problems. We had no pressure at all. The environment was slow-paced and laid back. I was happy. My husband's grandmother taught me how to make bread from scratch. This was done every morning at 4:00 am. Not being an early riser, I learned to adjust. We lived with his grandparents a few weeks before moving into our home. One night his grandfather asked us if we wanted "fish or chicken" for dinner. We told him chicken. Kentucky Fried sure sounded good. I started to set the table and heard this God-awful sound outside. Thinking, it was one of the children, I peeked out the window. There he was, Jake's granddad, with his white tee-shirt and dirty jean overalls. He was running around the back, with an ax in hand, trying to catch one of his chickens. I had fish.

As our stable life was established, I, once again, was becoming bored.

Even with a positive attitude towards life, I really missed drinking. Since I haven't drunk in 3 weeks, I knew it was under control. Jake had acquired his new drug connections, so I knew he didn't care. The kids had friends they played with the majority of times, so that was not an issue.

So I drank. A few weeks later, due to my inexcusable reasons for not being there and my lack of poor work habits, I lost my job. My self-confidence was lost again. I assumed that your employees were not allowed to drink on the job.

I did get another job, however. The name shall not be submitted because it was an exceptionally well reputable hotel. But I will say that the quality of work I performed in housekeeping there and my housekeeper's status was promoted to Head Lobby Attendant within the first week.

Someone must have recognized me as a high potential employee at the time. For at least a month, I had demonstrated a high level of expertise.

It was a lot of responsibly handed to me, so getting buzzed before work was a priority. One day at work, my supervisor pulled me in the backroom; we spoke about my job performance duties. She asked me a question that sounded way too familiar; she asked me if I had a drinking problem. "Do I have a drinking problem"? No, I said.

But I sure do have a problem with other people sticking there nose in my business, I thought to myself.

Jake just happened to show up right then. I collapsed in tears. A severe nervous breakdown was in the due process. Pleading with him to take me out of this terrible place, he did. These people had no idea the issues that had to be dealt with at home. They did not know my background whatsoever. Their accusation was daring. I never went back.

CRACK & ALCOHOL

Knowing I was in charge, I quit. Weeks went by, and I was miserable. Jake's addiction problems surfaced to an all-time high. Our electronics and jewelry made their way to the local pawn shop weekly. Since he didn't have a concern for our best interest, why should I? My consumption of alcohol escalated. Parties would last for days, as I had "new" friends now.

The children were more or less left to fend themselves at this age. I hardly knew where they played, and I didn't know where I was half the time.

Every day was a party that drifted in from the night before. Sleep was not an option anymore. It seemed as if my life was coming to an end, quite frankly, I didn't care. Jake's irresponsible actions caused him a dire consequence. Let's just say he had to go away for a little while. Not being able to make ends meet, anymore the children and I were facing eviction. Great! Here we go again. Going against their better judgment and my pleading, my parents agreed to take us in. I was extremely grateful to them. The urgency to move in a short time frame left many valuable items behind. At this time, it was of no concern.

When we all got settled in, rules and guidelines were made. The one, in particular, was "no drinking." I was happy to oblige.

BACK HOME

With our new life ahead of us, the children and I adapted well to our new surroundings. This time my decision to drink was final! Since it was my parents' home, I recognized their objectives to maintain control of the household. I was respecting their values once again. Besides, they were helping me seek new solutions to my problems. My reliably and trust issues with them were starting to become clearly defined again. It was my "new" beginning. Drinking and socializing didn't appeal to me anymore. Working two jobs did not allow any timeframe for such activities.

I tried extremely hard to feed and support my family, as they so desperately deserved. I could even afford the huge "troll" collection my daughter wanted. As far as my son was concerned, being outside, getting into mischief was "his" hobby. My father loved to tell stories to kids. In the wintertime, dad would tell the story of "Jack Frost." One summer, I heard my dad screaming outside.

"Who the hell got into the white paint"?! He yelled. Of course, we tried to locate my son. We found him with white paint all over his clothes. He asked him why he had painted the whole side of the shed. His reply; "I didn't do it!" "Jack Frost did"! How can you be mad at that? It was so funny. The tale lasted for years.

This was the first time in ages that I was assertively responsible as an individual.

Each day it got better. My natural energy and appetite for food were increasing as well. Everything in life was good. I was happy.

There was no way I had a drinking problem. For two months now, I had not one sip of alcohol and did it all by myself. Thank God. With my willpower and my well-deserved recognition, I had done it.

I had even started reading my bible again. There was a time in my youth, where I was so disgruntled with God, that I turned the "other" way. As I studied and read my "satanic" bible, I cursed and renounced him with every inch of my wellbeing. As a youth, curiosity found me dabbling in the occult with a "Quija board," as well.

May I give you some sound advice? These are NOT for entertainment "purpose only." When we were living in our mobile home, I contacted a 9-year old little girl; her name was "Nivea." I broke the board in half. I was "not" drinking at the time. My personal opinion now is that of such; this game board is a gateway to another dimension that I "will not" partake of.

THE SECRETS

Those months were great! My life had turned around. Then before I knew it, there was a drink in my hand. What happened? "I quit! I don't drink anymore, how did this get here?" As these thoughts tormented my mind, I could not grasp the concept of how, when, or where the alcohol was obtained.

My lack of self-respect and confidence resided once again with me. My parents had made a sacrifice and personal commitment to help us. I felt like a complete loser. I was so embarrassed and ashamed. The only action I could take was to keep it from them.

So, I developed strategic aims to do so.

It worked.

I had everything under control this time. It wasn't too much fun, because I had to drink secretly.

I thought, "what they didn't know wouldn't hurt them." For everyone not to know, I waited patiently until they went to bed. Or I waited until I got to work. This way, everyone would not suspect that I was drinking again.

My analytical plan of action worked.

I had 6-packs, and bottles stashed everywhere. In the house, they were in places that I didn't even know existed as a child growing up.

Behind local stores and neighborhood trash cans were my favorite areas.

Before long, my job performance started to suffer. I honestly can not recall whether I quit or was terminated from both jobs. Nothing seemed to matter anymore. "What was going on in my mind, and why couldn't I stop drinking"? I knew I wasn't an alcoholic, but "maybe" I had a small drinking problem. Not having an effective resolution, left me confused. This terrible substance left me feeling like I was a horrible person.

I know "how" I got like this. My parents could not reinforce positive behavior. It was Jake's fault for being an addict and allowing his family to fall apart. It was the children's lack of obedience towards me. Most of all, it was the world that had denied me from birth.

There is nobody in the whole universe that neither loves nor cares for me. And God, there was no God. If there was, he surely wasn't here. Of course, I stopped reading my bible.

All of my friends had deserted me. Most of all, my children hated me, and I was left feeling isolated from everyone. I was not happy.

IM NOT A DRUNK

The world around me started to evolve with new technology, as it was in the early '90s. Practically drinking every waking moment of each day, I felt invisible. Every day the recollection of conversations was becoming apparent to my mother and father. My dad had suffered previous heart conditions. My mother said that one day he would have a stroke, and it would be my fault. Several weeks after that, my father and I were arguing with each other concerning my drinking habits. He had a major stroke. He survived with major disabilities. Try living with that guilt. It hurt me so profoundly that I might have been the cause of effect it had on him.

It took many years for me to have a complete resolution to this matter. Knowing that my dad had medical issues, my conduct did not help at that time.

My mother never knew how deeply sorry I was.

My mother had to give much care and attention to my father, because of the incident, so she decided it was best we left. At the time, I could not rationalize how she could throw us out in the street. Looking back, her response was rational. She was fed up. Quite frankly, so was I. She handed me $100 and provided hotel expenses for one week. I had drunk so much that week; it left me in a state of dramatic disorientation. The feelings that were felt were unimaginable, even for me, at this time. Knowing that we needed to find shelter soon, I called a friend of the family. My family graciously drove us to the bus station. Off we went, headed for Georgia.

Our adjustment was good for the first week. I found a local movie theatre that sold beer. So I was happy. The living conditions were pitiful there. His home was actually more disorganized than "my" previous ones.

Being that he was 650lbs and solely remained in his chair, might have been the just cause of his untidiness.

His intolerance with my drinking habits led our conversations to arguments. The kids and I decided to get even with him. After we cooked his dinner, one dozen eggs to be exact. My sophisticated skill for originality was eager to assert itself. We spiked his ice tea with fourteen "Pepto Bismol" tablets. Let's just say, the children and I had to find alternatives for going to the bathroom. He never knew.

After this display of misconduct, our conflicts became more frequent.

It was a month later that he wanted us to leave. This time, I was more than willing to seek residence elsewhere.

THE HOMELESS SHELTER

As I was in the process of gathering our belongings, my friend Dolly, demonstrated a willingness to help us. This time she was non-judgmental, and her sincere gesture of kindness was accepted. She used her personal resources to get us placed in a local Woman's shelter back home, near my parents. The one condition that I didn't like was; no drinking allowed because they would test me.

I agreed to all of the rules and regulations. Dolly took care of the proper paperwork, and arrangements were made for us to arrive back home. Besides, I was starting to miss my family. I knew they were ashamed of me at this time. I believed they could not truly love me.

Looking back, it was "my" inability to receive it.

For some odd reason, Dolly desperately tried to show her affection towards me. Our friendship had become so distant at this time; I wanted us to make amends with each other. I needed a friend. All I had ever done was hurt her feelings. The idea of her wanting to remain friends must have had a hidden motive. That was not the case. My recollection of my past mistakes left one of hurt and pain towards others. The most damage that was apparent was done to my parents and children.

I wasn't too happy about living in a homeless shelter. But Dolly had already put in an application for "low-income housing." She had an effective way of transforming thoughts into action. A month rolled by, and still no word about the apartment. I was able to maintain a high degree of self-control and managed to stay sober. My appetite for food came back, as once before. Being sober was bringing some positive results into my life.

We had a roof over our heads, clean clothes, and food in our stomach. Now, we did have to wipe our butts with socks. Money was lacking at times; therefore, we could not afford toilet paper. My conversations and interactions with my parents were brief, however friendly.

I patiently awaited the news concerning the apartment. Feeling a little antsy, a small part of me wanted to drink. Everyone around me had tried so hard to help. I felt letting them down now, would be a critical mistake. This time I was committed to assume responsibility for my family. It was about time. My parents deserved to have a loving daughter that they had raised.

My children also desperately needed a mother to guide their growth process. Most of all, I needed direction to be a more productive individual. All of the thoughts I had of past failures and disappointments made me feel miserable. However, I did not drink. I couldn't, not with the consistent alcohol tests.

Then out of the blue, it happened! The letter of acceptance for our apartment had arrived in the mail.

Thoughts of drinking were eliminated.

I was so happy that the children and I were finally getting our own place. I cried profusely. The excitement I felt made me never want to drink again.

We soon packed our belongings and moved in. The housing was surprisingly acceptable to raise small children. This was my opportunity to focus on stabilizing a suitable environment for my children finally. I was delighted.

In the beginning, we didn't have a whole lot of material possessions. My parents provided furniture and most of the essential items that we needed. With my creative nature, I assembled furniture that was gathered together from the trash dumpster. Of course, these items were supplied from my 11-year-old son.

He thought they were treasures. I guess he was right. My son and I had still remained extremely close, despite everything. The relationship with my 13-year-old daughter was becoming distant. Being that she was becoming a teenager, I backed off a little.

I still monitored her whereabouts, just from a distance. She had excelled in her studies in school, and even at an early age, I trusted her judgment. My son, on the other hand, had no regard for school whatsoever. His lack of concentration and the ability to focus on any given task weakened his learning abilities. Recognizing his exceptionally creative and artistic abilities made up for this.

My practical spending habits allowed me to manage a household on a $381 a month welfare check. We had no car and an allowance of $240 a month food stamps. It was hard, but I pulled it off. It was at this time, around one year that Jake arrived back north and resided with his family. I wanted to seek his help with the finances. I tried to reach him by phone one day. His mother answered the phone and explained to me that he had his "own problems" and didn't want to help out. Therefore, the children were my sole responsibility. With this incompetent reaction that I got, put me on a mission to use my abilities to their fullest. The inner strength that was given to me was incredible. So, I took on that responsibility.

Being sober for months now, I was effectively able to communicate with others. My personal hygiene and appearance were becoming important to me once again.

The confidence that I was displaying made a positive impact on my parents and children. DSS was watching me very close, making sure I was giving appropriate care for the children, so I "knew" I couldn't drink now.

It had been months since my last drink, God, I knew all along I was right. The willpower was inside me all along! Everyone had the wrong impression of me. I "didn't" have a drinking problem.

However, in my quiet thoughts, the urge was still there. I never expressed my thoughts. I didn't drink.

For about six months now, we started to live our lives to the fullest.

This time I had everything under control. God had given me a new source of empowerment to take control of my life.

I was given another chance to prove myself to others. My acceptance and belonging that I had always yearned for as a child was finally achieved.

This was so very important for me.

I was happy.

Then, something happened. I still, to this day, don't know how I picked up a drink. I was drunk.

The recollection of that day remains a blur. But I do recall, not having feelings of shame nor guilt. There was no remorse because I "deserved" to be miserable this time. My complicated life and the inability to make sound decisions would never become a reality to me. This time, my skilled competence for drinking in secrecy came to a halt. I finally gave in for my much-needed desire to drink.

My daily drinking habits consisted of; 1 pint of Jack Daniels, or vodka (being my favorite), and a 12-pack, to a beer case. When the results were optimized, I would buy another fifth of vodka.

OUT OF CONTROL

As I continued on a rampage of self-destruction, something seemed to be different this time. After the consumption of 1 or 2 drinks, I could not remember where I was. Being that I never left the house, it was always on the couch. My desire to drink was greater than my household responsibilities.

Somehow the house maintained upkeep.

My 13-year-old daughter, being able to achieve positive results at any given task level, probably did it. At the time, my strong commitment to exceptional housekeeping did not matter. The children and my parents had become a figment of my imagination.

I had no remorse for my actions.

The acceptance of my life had become a reality. This was it, and I started to give up. There was no more energy inside of me to even attempt to try. All I wanted to do was drink. The obsession became greater as a few weeks passed. However, the strong desire to drink was starting to make me feel uncomfortable. Even with the large consumptions of alcoholic beverages, I was unable to achieve my desired results. When I drank, my upper arms and hands began to tremble. Thoughts of quitting again started to develop. To lose my motor functions, was not part of my plan.

Recognizing that I might have a problem, I quickly decided to stop. There was a small problem; I could not. Knowing that it would probably kill me, as it had become like breathing air.

When I "was" sober, I felt intoxicated.

When I drank, alcohol gave me an adverse effect. Leaving me in a state of a "zombie," and significantly impaired. I felt like a "ship in a bottle." My well-established place was that of my couch. Sitting there for hours on end just staring, guess I was waiting for my ghostly image friends to come back to me. One day I got up to get another drink from the refrigerator. It was three days later.

As the life I once knew, the hardships, mistakes, insecurities, and even my fondness memories seemed to disappear.

The feeling of the world closing in on me was becoming my reality. It was a challenging task to consume food because my body was starting not to digest it anymore. My persistent actions of vomiting occurred daily. The lack of food was apparent because it consisted mostly of liquid. The tortuous effect that this had on me was unbearable. I thought once again, "Where the hell is God"?

My inability to perceive time left me wondering whether it was day or night. It didn't matter. Having acquired the feelings of undesired desolation, I wanted to cease to exist.

These emotions intensified every day.

It was as Satan "himself" had implanted a seed of self-destruction deep inside of me, and I was cursed for all eternity.

His demons tormented me every night, as I guzzled my vodka and beer. Their consistent visual appearance and haunting communication with me, left me paralyzed, to remain seated on the couch. I had no choice. "This is how you are going to die, deal with it," they would tell me. "This is your destiny, and the only way out of your pain"; "You will die here, with a drink in your hand." This happened every night for one week. It was becoming clear this was the case. I had no reason to live.

One morning I had awakened in my bed.

There was a man beside me. My strong urge of curiosity startled him.

He awoke and spoke to me. To my surprise, I had no recollection of who this person was. Upon the conversation, I realized that he only had one tooth dangling from his top gums.

My mind could not perceive the incident that took place. I graciously asked him to please leave. It greatly upset me.

MY LAST GLANCE

I was becoming emotionally terrified at this time. "What is happening to me"? I thought to myself. "Am I dying"? The awareness of my resistance to change was starting to become evident. The pain was so great; I "had to get drunk.

As I sat there that night, my images of demons were nonexistent. Being alone, there was time to focus solely on my thoughts. Because I indeed had a drinking problem, and couldn't stop, I knew the problem must be resolved. Maybe it was too late. Having a feeling of absolute disgust for myself, I wanted to die. So I drank, and drank, and drank.

As I sat there that night, and it was a very long night. I somehow could recall past events in my life. As a child, a teenager, and as an adult, memories were starting to surface. My parents, the most loving human beings alive, were always there for me—my hopes and dreams as a young child. The security and warmth I felt growing up.

My awkwardness as a teen that made it impossible for me to fit in. Financial burdens and problems that Jake and I had in the past. Even blame that was placed on him for breaking our family apart was in my thoughts. But most of all, the thoughts of my children were indeed the love of my life. We had been through so much together.

Even though I was very drunk by now, my mind could rationalize the reality of my life. We had two bedrooms. I resided in one room, which allowed the children to occupy the much larger bedroom. Stumbling through the long hallway, I went to check on children. They were, of course, sound asleep by this time, being that the time was around 3:30 am. I tucked them in and took one last look at them. I was at peace, knowing this was my last night alive.

In my heart, I knew that all their pain and suffering would cease when I died. There would be a brief time before they would soon forget me, and their hopelessness of life would soon disappear. They deserved a better life than this one. I stood over them for a few minutes; I tried to envision their future.

It was one of happiness, stability, love, and hope. With the love of a mother, that would guide them through the rest of their lives. I loved them with all my heart and was willing to die for them. They had new clothes and toys which they deserved to have.

It broke my heart that I could not be there to watch them grow up. But it was inevitable. That night was my last. As I proceeded to walk away, it was not my intention to look back. When I got to the doorway, I froze. There was an apparent, unexplainable force that prevented me from moving. Not realizing what was happening, I turned my head slightly to see if the kids were okay.

They were still asleep. I was able to turn back around in the doorway.

My hands still clenched to each side, as it was holding me up. I looked again at the children. I was remembering when I had held them for the first time, and counting their little tiny toes and fingers, to make sure they were all accounted for. I remembered their first smile, their first steps, and their first words. The visions that were seen had been lost in my memory somehow. I thought to myself, of how I had promised them, at birth, my love would always be there for them, no matter what. With tears pouring from my eyes, the mobility to move again, and walk away released itself. Sitting back once more on my couch, I continued to cry. I need God.

It was dark but visible.

As I sat there and drank for a short period, tears continued, with great feelings of remorse. As I slowly looked up in front of me, on the wall, there was a picture of Christ. I had always been a born-again Christian most of my adult life. Nothing mattered at this moment other than how I had let him down. I kept starring at the picture, accepting the end of my life with forgiveness. I cried more. I took a few more drinks, just waiting for his response to take me back.

When I glared again and looked at him, it appeared as if he had tears rolling down his cheeks.

At that moment, there was a feeling of electric shock running through my body. I fell to the ground and cried like "never" before. With my knees placed firmly on the carpet, and my hands stretched up, I screamed to my God, to please help me! This time it was him and me. I had nothing to live for. Pleading, praying, and crying for his help. "I am in pain, and I am dying!"; "I want to live and not die a slow death!" "I want to stop drinking, but I can't!" I repeatedly screamed at him.

That night I cried myself to sleep.

When I awoke later in the afternoon, with my puffy eyes and body suffering the effects of the worst hangover that I had ever experienced, my day started. But thoughts of having a drink were not there. This was unusual. The realization that I finally admitted there was a drinking problem relieved me. So what now? Having my faith in God, rejuvenated once again, I waited. "Faith as little as a mustard seed," I thought to myself.

GOD SHOWED UP

A few hours had passed by, all day, my cheerfulness prevailed. The kids were outside playing for the most part, except periodic entries of thirst control. Early that evening, there was a knock at the door. They were missionaries from a local church. At this time, I was eager to listen. After sitting in the living room talking for a brief period, they relayed to me their church. You almost had to pick me up with a shovel. It was the place of worship, the Christian school/church of my early childhood education. My response was silence. I just looked up and smiled. That night, the awareness that the incident took place was denied. But, I knew deep down, it did.

The next morning was productive.

The kids with their friends at the time were once again outside. Looking back, the belief was, they wanted to keep a distance from me.

After a few hours of housecleaning, there was a knock at the door. I opened the door, standing in the hallway, was a friend I had not seen in ages, an old drinking buddy. Going against my better judgment, I invited him in for a drink. My mother's hospitable ways had always taught me to be also. We had coffee. We sat on my tarnished couch in the living and talked for some time. Noticing that he didn't bring any beer, as he previously had done in the past, I never said anything. My concern and hesitancy of letting him in was this factor. I was happy.

Finally, the personal experience that I had the night before had to be shared with someone. The comfort that was felt with this individual made it possible. So I told him. He also shared a similar story that happened to him in previous months. Now I understood why he had arrived without beer.

He stopped drinking. This time I looked up, with my keen wit, I winked.

With curiosity in mind, I listened to what he had to say. His reinforcement with positive behavior was appealing to me. We had always been great drinking buddies, but this was different.

Throughout the conversation, connectivity with him was greatly producing. We just thought the same, laughed about situations and problems that would make a priest drink. The comic relief made me feel almost normal again, and I wasn't drinking.

We ended up sitting there for hours.

He asked if I wanted to go for a drive since it was summer, the kids were okay, stuck in the house, and mentally drained from the previous night, I obliged. Fresh air sounded like a great idea.

My friend and I went for a long drive.

We laughed about past failures and random disappointments in our life, as well as the fondest memories we had.

Still unable to rationalize the bond of closeness we were starting to establish; my mind was intrigued. It sparked enthusiasm within me when he shared personal information. These stories, however, seemed way too familiar, about my own life.

Everything he spoke of is that I could relate, left me in awe.

As we proceeded with our short road trip, I found myself in the area, was Jake and I had lost our first home.

When I looked out the window, there was the church where Jake and I had been saved and had a membership. Acting on compulsion, I asked my friend to turn in the driveway. This time, I soberly walked in, looking for someone, anyone to pray with me. In bible study, some women came out and responded to my needs. I explained to them my situation at hand.

Going into the auditorium after, I quietly got down on my knees and prayed. There wasn't much light. However, I knew my way around. Looking up at where I had been baptized, I cried.

Still quiet, with soft tears in my eyes, I humbly asked for forgiveness, and to please help me".

Kneeling there only briefly, just to gain my composure, I got up. By the time I had gotten back to the exit door, my tears had been wiped away. I felt at peace, but I knowingly seemed to have a major drinking problem. All I knew at that time was, all I had to rely on was my trust with God. What else did I have? Something stirred in me, and I knew something was about to happen.

As I got back in my friend's vehicle, he noticed that I had been crying. Asking me if I was alright, my reply was, "I didn't know yet." He looked at me and smiled. I wanted to go home. In the last few days, I was developing a strong power of recall. It was motivating, yet it terrified me. Part of me wanted to drink, the other significant driving force in me wanted to stop. So, I drank.

The coffee was cold; therefore, I asked if we could stop to get another one.

We went back to the house, still talking, still laughing. I, of course, invited him in. The need for companionship was much desired, especially at this time in my life.

I still felt alone and hopeless.

My friend asked me a question; "Do I and the kids want to go to a meeting"? I, of course, using my common sense, and judging from our conversation that day, I "knew" what he meant.

COMING TO TERMS

It was one of those "radical" 12-step group meetings. I had always heard of those. This conceptual idea came from my parents, friends, strangers, Dolly, and even my 11 and 13-year-old children. Okay, "I said," the day had been tiring yet made me receptive to new ideas of change.

I had given up and was just so exhausted. There had to be an alternate course of action to take. This point in my life, if I couldn't stop drinking, I would at least listen to the sound advice of others.

Sitting in his car outside the building, there were grave concerns and wondered what I was getting myself into.

When we walked through the front door, hands shaking, I turned around to leave, just as that hit me, a group of people walked in and caused me to change direction. It pushed me even further towards the room where the meeting was.

"Okay," I thought to myself. What the hell. As I cautiously proceeded to enter the room, there was the alertness of my surroundings that had not been demonstrated in a very long time. We sat down, this time I was in the back, of course.

Throughout the next hour, I paid close attention to what was being said. I observed and tried to analyze every individual in that room.

At first, judging by appearances and their confidence in speaking, I thought I was in the wrong place. The atmosphere was that of; a professional office board meeting. I listened, some laughed, and others shed tears when they openly communicated and discussed their most intimate stories. For the first and the only time in life, the sense of belonging resided in me. For the first time in a very long time, I felt needed, honest, and real. These people were doctors, lawyers, teachers, young kids, women, men, office workers, and construction workers, just to name a few.

We had nothing in common; at least that was my perception.

As the end of the meeting was drawing near, the speaker asked, "does anyone have anything they would like share"?

I looked up at my friend, who was sitting across the room from me. He looked straight into my eyes and nodded with a friendly gesture. I was seated, with both arms stretched over the back of the chairs beside me. Sitting beside me were my children, my daughter to the left, and my son on the right.

My arms had been stretched out, placing my hands directly on their shoulders. Overwhelmed by emotion, my stomach dropped to the floor. This is where "God" took charge. I looked to my right and then slowly to my left; I saw my children's faces, tears in their eyes, and mine. My once clenched fingers on their small shoulders released themselves. I let go.

As the speaker; was getting ready to announce his final words, I stood up abruptly. I said the following words; "my name is Cheryl, and I am a suffering alcoholic, please help me." It was in an instant these words were said; that every solitary cell of my being had collected together and put back into place. The pieces of the puzzle had been put together. My acceptance that I was sick with a disease, and it was called; "alcoholism," was finally admitted.

Finally, after 19 years of drinking, I came to terms with acceptance. I am an alcoholic.

SELF AWARENESS

With this new conscious awareness and acceptance, my life was starting to make sense. I was able to rationalize, through my hazy mind, that my parents were not to blame for my drinking. My upbringing was not the cause. The ongoing positive reinforcements for me were always there. They always used positive imagery to set an example for me.

I was clothed, fed, and had a more than a suitable roof over my head. My mother had sacrificed her personal life to be a homemaker. My father held a high degree of professional expertise. I wanted for nothing. It was not the children's fault. All they had tried to do in life at this time was, try to deal effectively with anticipated stressful situations. It also was not because of Jake. He tried to be a good father; however, his addictions made it impossible for him. My mother-in-law at the time tried to give us support and guidance. To this day, I cannot express the gratitude that I have towards my friend Dolly. She had always stood beside me.

After the meeting, we all went home. I had stopped crying and was relieved. My friend and I engaged in a brief conversation before he left. He explained to me, if I felt like drinking, call someone. The side kept the numbers I had retrieved at all times. He also told me, "go to meetings." I did. I went two, three, a day. Our paths never crossed again.

So here was my life at the age of 31. This time I was willing to listen to others that had walked before me.

Soon they were beside me. I can not elaborate on what was said; protecting the organization, its members, and their amenity. But I will say this; I was accepted.

For the first time, "real" friends were in my life. Knowing that I could rely on support and guidance, my trust was becoming solid again. There was still confused with my thoughts, and my hands shook quite a lot.

My comprehension of verbal understanding was slightly altered also. I was told, "it would pass" It did.

Several weeks had passed. I didn't drink. I had met one woman, petite in stature, articulately soft-spoken and kind. She made a favorable impression. After hearing her speak many times of her life experience, I gained a lot of respect for her. I chose her to teach and guide me through my new sobriety.

Her positive attitude towards life made a significant impact on mine.

She had the life that I had only dreamt of for my family. A beautiful home, dedicated husband, a well stabilized little girl, and credible employment, and most of all, she "really" looked happy. I wanted that! I hung on to that woman like you wouldn't believe.

We had many conversations in my home. The children continued to stay distant from me. I didn't blame them. Besides, this was important to me. This time, however, I did care of their whereabouts. The bond with my woman friend was starting to become a close relationship. It was in these weeks when my self-esteem was coming back. This was when I started to recognize that maybe, the potential to manage my life was indeed feasible. My self-worth was strengthened with these thoughts. That may be, God did have a plan and a purpose for me. He had always been there. I chose to look away. I found God.

Weeks went by, and they turned into months. The physical ability to maintain my household was returning.

My relationship with my parents and children was beginning to build trust. However, the kids could not understand why I was at meetings "all" the time. On the other hand, they were happy I was sober. I chose to take on the responsibility of arranging and assembling coffee at my favorite meeting. I was still on welfare at the time. Therefore, I had time to attend numerous meetings a day.

Lack of education cost me decent employment. Jake was still not helping financially at this time. My mother would help with transportation as needed. The store was close enough to walk to. That is when the funds were available. My son's eleventh birthday, we had one blue frosted cupcake, with one candle, we split in 3 ways. It was memorable.

A few painstakingly months passed by, it was a long summer.

The unwanted desire to drink was ceasing. My ability to live responsibly sober was a difficult task. Learning to have positive responses to challenging situations was tough. Also, learning to keep an even temperament was almost impossible. I was told, "this would pass."

In my "drinking world," there was; feelings of hatred, anger, fear, loneliness, resent, shame, guilt, and distrust. However, my newfound sobriety, I had found; kindness, compassion, hope, belief, trust, loyalty, and, most of all, love. I was starting to remember all of the pain that had an impact on others. This left me in tears at each meeting. The numbing effect of alcohol was starting to diminish.

Therefore, my real emotions and feelings were producing. I was happy to feel "something." There was a long road ahead.

A few months had passed. My memory is still quite unclear about specific events. However, one remains embedded. To see a friend of mine intoxicated. With chronic alcoholism full-blown, I had the displeasure of seeing "myself" sober. Being face to face with this individual, humbled, and encouraged me to move forward even more diligently. I thought to myself, "I never want to go back this again, ever."

MY GED DIPLOMA

Maintaining a positive outlook on life, I decided to go back to school and obtain my GED. The fact was an 8th-grade education was not acceptable for decent employment. My children deserved more than what they were accustomed to. My family was incredibly supportive. Three times a week, walking a half an hour each way, sometimes in the rain, I completed the course.

Five months had gone by. I was sober. My parental responsibilities were strengthening. The relationship with my parents was building trust once again, as well as the children. They had sat me down and told me how proud they all were that I was not drinking. This event was a significant stepping-stone in my recovery process. It was because of their support; I was growing stronger and became humble before God.

It was also in this time, four friends that I had acquired, passed away. There was one, an individual who had a little over twenty-three sobriety. Ironically, coming home one night alone, which was "never" the case, was hit by a drunk driver. There was a girl in her early twenties with a small child, suicide by gun, instant death. A woman in her mid-thirties took her boyfriend's pistol, placed it in her mouth, and pulled the trigger, instant death by suicide.

A close, intimate, ex-boyfriend of mine took a gun and placed it to his head and shot himself in the head. My hatred for alcohol started to develop. I educated myself with alcoholism and abuse.

It was now in the early '90s. I am now thirty-two years old. My half-year sobriety date is approaching close. Making amends to the people that have been harmed by my inappropriate behavior is on my list.

The willingness to do so was of great importance to me. It was the year 1995 when President Bill Clinton resided. We will "not" go there. The fashion era was becoming that of colorful and loose-fitting clothing. The Mitsubishi Roamer was one of the popular cell phones of its day. It weighed approximately 200 pounds. The phone didn't weigh that much, just felt that way.

After making my amends to several individuals, it was time for my immediate family. This was going to be a difficult task. After an honest and long-winded conversation, I asked for forgiveness. To my surprise, they graciously had accepted the apology.

Then, it was the hard one, my children.

Individually I spoke with them.

There were "too" many reasons to say, "I am sorry." Therefore, I said, "I am sorry for everything I have ever done and everything that I never could do." When it was resolved between us, we hugged, tears rolling down our cheeks.

As for Dolly, my only friend who never let me down; she just wanted "me" back.

Unconditional love is what "that" is called. Some amends were denied, but I had to make them anyway. There were also many events, "too" severe to share. The "cat" incident; was written down on paper and ripped to shreds!

MY FATHERS PASSING

With great enthusiasm, I was encouraged to be almost six months sober.

My parents were residing in sunny central Florida, as they did every winter. They passed their cares away with a place in Ocean City, Maryland, by the bay. My mother had phoned me one day. I was so excited to talk to her. She explained to me that my father was in the hospital and that he had another stroke.

It was not good. He had a long history of heart disease, and the last stroke was about a year ago. This was his second. My father is a strong man; I knew he would pull through this. Then my mother proceeded to tell me the reality. "He is 99.9% brain dead and will not functionally recover", she said. I understood.

My dad did not have a living will; therefore, the decision had to be made, from my mother. With emotional support from the family, it was decided to let him go in peace. He would have wanted us to. The day set was February 14th. It was Valentine's Day. Lack of funds and fear of losing sobriety prevented me from making arrangements to fly down.

A few days had passed, and it was finally the 14th of February. I needed to be not alone that day. Mom was to call when the procedure was over. We did not know what time, so it was a long afternoon. It was a critical situation that almost put me over the edge. My newly acquired friend, from my meetings, spent the day with me.

She understood my feelings of despair.

We went to a local restaurant to have something to eat. I could not.

We engaged in constant conversation for hours. In one moment, I looked up at the sky. The scenic image is still recalled in my mind. The clouds parted slowly, allowing a stream of lights, beam down on the horizon. At this instant, an intense feeling of calmness and love shattered through my body.

I knew my father had passed at that moment. God had released his tired body and set his spirit free.

I expressed the feelings to my friend; "he's gone," I told her. We continued our conversation with much compassion on her part. Then, I drank. I called the waitress over and asked her; may I have another cup, as my coffee had gotten cold by that time". I felt God's presence.

My father had not only given me another steppingstone but gave me more reason to live. I never knew "how" much I loved him until that moment. This was his time for rewards, of unchanged kindness towards others.

I was grateful that I was sober and had made my amends; this strengthened me beyond words. The only regrets were not spending enough time with him, my choice. Not being the daughter that he had deserved. The only positive consequence was, I did not drink.

The hatred I had of alcohol and the disease of alcoholism was apparent to everyone around me. However, respect for being powerless over it made me closer to God. As my higher power was starting to heal the inside, my body showed signs of appropriate grooming.

My recollection of events was still quite hazy at this time.

However, two extraordinary memories brought compelling life changes.

At the end of March of that year, I received my high school diploma in the mail. I was 32 years old. I cried.

Near the end of the year, I walked across the stage and was handed my degree. You better believe my head was up, and my eyes looked straight forward.

Unfortunately, I almost tripped down a short flight of stairs coming down because of that. I was happy.

Shortly after that, on August 14, 1995, I celebrated my one-year sobriety. There are no words to express my feelings that night.

STARTING OVER

My short-term personal accomplishments had been attained. I had recognized my parental responsibilities and was maintaining a positive role model for my children. I was starting to have self-respect and confidence. My perception of reality was starting to change.

However, there were times when my immature emotional stability would present itself. I was told, 'this too shall pass".

My drinking started when I was 13; therefore, my mentality was that of an early teen. Surprisingly so, the thought of drinking was not desired anymore. The inability to adjust emotionally, accept others, and situations beyond my control were my "problem." It made me think, 'know why I started drinking in the first place". That was a "bad" joke.

 Life seemed to have past me by, and someone threw me in this changing environment.

Sometimes I would just sit and weep, no reason, just because. The outbreaks would adjust themselves in time, I was told. The uncomfortable feelings were nothing in comparison to the 19 years of drinking that were left behind. So, I decided to be consistent with meetings, and a network of great friends, to maintain my sobriety. This period of my life is still disoriented. However, before I could blink, one year and six months went by.

I was sober.

I continued with my meetings still twice a day. It was now, me helping others, as much as a could. I knew my limitations, however, because I was still a learning instrument.

There were times of tremendous, overwhelming joy emotions. The need for reprogramming my thought patterns, action, and reaction to life was much needed. Its new trial and tribulations placed me in an emotional whirlwind. No matter what my willingness to do my part remained unchanged.

CONSTRICTED FUNDS

During my first year and a half, my attendance was regular at meetings.

The purposeful self-attention had been achieved, and it was time to consider gainful employment. Being on welfare for a few years was going to come to an end. Undoubting, the high school diploma that was just acquired was not sufficient enough to obtain a decent job. Nowadays, in the 2010s, you have to have a high school diploma to work at McDonald's.

Homelife was becoming pleasant once more. The times spent with mom, and the kids, at her beach house in Ocean City were the most memorable. I remember many times, my son and I went crabbing on her peer. His responsibility was to catch them in the net as they pulled them up, one by one, with the fishing pole. We would sit there for hours and talk. I never could cook them, however. That task was given to my mother. The screams of the crabs cooking made me unable to eat them. I have a problem eating something that had been looking at me. Besides, just being able to have a meaningful relationship with my son, once again, meant the world to me. My daughter, now being 13, was in her own space. She had always displayed a mature attitude; therefore, I left her alone. I understood how she felt. My son, I kept close to me. We were inseparable. We had a very close bond together at this time.

Having recognized the need for inward change, my attempts for further self-discipline were ongoing. It was now time to take on financial responsibility for my family. Jake's inability to help provide funds for his family still was a problem for us. He refused to spend time with kids, and I needed a positive male role model for them. They needed reinforcements from another viewpoint. The application form "Big Brothers and Sisters" was accepted. With tedious research, they found a suitable match. They were happy. At one time, I had to lawfully enforce visitation with him, because I was so tired having "all" the responsibility. I was forced to obtain child support for the children. This, unfortunately, dropped my welfare check of $381 a month to $0.

The government must have assumed that his $30 a week child support check was better suited. My food stamps were also cut in half. This was a "productive" decision. We were dirt poor at this time, but we were happy. But, I could always practically approach problems. This was going to be no different.

There was a hurdle to cross over. My mother's helping hand always produced more than expected, with money and food. We still had no car. The children deserved to have new clothes, and toys to play with. The responsibility to do so was no longer an option. Sometimes, there was not enough food for all of us; therefore, I went without. There was always food for them, except for the holiday season that year.

THE GOOD SON

I had just arrived home from a meeting; the children were sitting on the couch. I greeted them and proceeded to make dinner. Upon opening the kitchen cabinets, to my dismay, "all" of the canned goods had disappeared. "What the hell happened to all the food," I screamed. My son, with his head down, approached me. "People from a church came by, they needed food for poor people, mommy," he reluctantly said. "Honey was poor," I explained to him. Now, what are "we" going to do for food"? I cried.

After going into my bedroom, still, in tears, I thought of what to do. I knew that my son's intentions were good, but how could he have given them "all" our food given to us? We had nothing to eat. Then, I recalled, when we had just moved back in with mom and dad. We had nothing. My family and I were walking on a street in D.C., museum visiting. We passed a group of homeless individuals. As I kept going, something made me turn around.

They're sitting in a big, brown box, was a woman. I briefly looked at her, and she as well. When I looked into her eyes, something touched my heart. I reached in my pocket, and grabbed all 65 cents that I owned, and gave it to her.

I went back to my son, still sitting on the couch, upset, grabbed him by the arms, and said, "I love you, you are very special". I let it go. My mother provided more food for us. I overlooked his sincere act of giving.

A week later, there was a knock at the door. I opened it. There were two ladies from an organization standing there in front of me. Three boxes resided in the hallway. I told them we had already given food, as I jokingly told them what my son had previously done. They said, "You don't understand; this is for you." Confusingly I told them they must have the wrong address. They verified my name. Someone had placed us on a list for a Thanksgiving meal. I was, for the first time in my life, speechless.

The food not only replaced what had been given away, but it was also more than could be put in the refrigerator. I was more than grateful to the anonymous sender, for "that" Thanksgiving was memorable. We never found out who the individual was.

A few weeks had passed, and Christmas was approaching faster each day.

There were minimal funds for gifts.

However, I knew something would come to mind with my never-ending resourcefulness to make it a great holiday.

Three days before Christmas, no gifts, I became discouraged. The phone rang. An organization was playing "secret Santa." The children had been invited to spend Christmas Eve at a party with pizza, soda, and Santa. There were going to be hundreds of new toys, for them to pick from, all they could carry.

Of course, I agreed to let them go.

The arrangements were made for transportation. The conversation was brief, as I had to regain my composure at that time. I had cried. My disbelief that this was happening left me in a state of awe.

When the children came back in from playing outside, I told them.

Their reaction was that of excitability.

Later that evening, there were still leftovers that I had frozen from Thanksgiving. Dinner was being prepared. Someone knocked at our door. I had asked my son to answer because my hands were full. He opened the door. "Mom,"! He yelled. "You need to come here." "What now?" I thought. I peeked around the corner, which gave me a plain view of our company. Standing there again, were two women with three boxes.

This time I had enough food to give.

I told them to hold on, as I started to gather non-perishable items that I had leftover. They pushed their way in and asked what I was doing. Well, it was apparent I was making dinner. They placed the heavy boxes on my counter.

"This is for you"! One woman said.

Trying to remain in solid control of my emotions was unattainable.

We had received yet another gesture of someone's kindness.

We had enough food in our home, to feed the children for a month. The cabinets were full, and the abundance of fresh food could almost not be placed in the refrigerator. I thanked them from the bottom of my heart. When they abruptly left, I had to go to my room. As I sat there in shock, tears rolling down my cheeks, I could not comprehend how these holidays were produced with a great victory. Then I looked up and cried even more. This miracle could have only come from one source.

These extraordinary domino falling events that had taken place were not of my imaginable ability. There was a divine intervention that made our holiday season grand. It was God.

Looking back now, I would highly appreciate the knowledge of the individual who made it possible for my children to have one of the best Christmas they ever had. Please recognize that your act of kindness is just when you contribute charitable items for the needy. A person's outlook in life may be changed forever. Thank you for doing this.

THE TURNING POINT

The holidays passed quickly, as they had arrived. We had a new beginning, as the year 1996 came in.

The food soon disappeared. My ongoing reality of not being able to support the children persisted. With my profound confidence now, a plan had to take effect.

Everything was falling into place.

I had even started to date again, for the first time in many years. After a few insignificant tries, for finding the right companion, I had met someone.

My children were hesitant at first with me dating but accepted the fact that I was happy and had a new boyfriend. My son, of course, got jealous.

Each day I was becoming stronger than the one before. The effectiveness to divide and delegate household duties among the children and me was good. With everything under control at home, and the kids being able to responsibly not need a sitter, the search to seize all opportunities began.

Not having the proper skills to obtain an office job was off the list. Even though I had an Administrative Specialist degree from my previous military training, technology was beginning to evolve at this time. We had no PC's back then, but the new age was beginning to surface. The available home computers were quite costly. My over qualifications, to work in the short-order field, was not enough to keep my head above water

THE STRIPPER SAGA

I had remembered a day, a jacket, with a business logo on the front.

The woman wearing it was an acquaintance of mine. We had spoken many times before, and she had been pleasant to talk with. Being curious, I asked for information about employment. She was a waitress at an "Exotic Dance Club."

They were accepting applications for exotic dance performers.

Never in my wildest dreams would I have imagined that life would place me here. A few days before, my son had gone into our freezer at home and could not even pull out two ice trays. With that thought and an open mind, I decided to check it at least out. Besides, never being in a strip club before, except when I was forced to go at 16, provoked my sense of inquiry. I thought, "What do I have to lose"?

She took me that very night, as I was eager to find gainful employment. We walked in, and she introduced me to the manager. My impression, at first, was one of awkwardness.

After our half an hour conversation, my reluctant attitude had changed. This place of the establishment was nothing in comparison to what I had envisioned.

The old sayings, "don't believe everything you see on TV." Best fits how I felt. The club was clean and served "no" alcohol. It was a juice bar. That was enticing for my sobriety; therefore, I auditioned with my careful observation of the friendly atmosphere. That night I came home with an abundance of money. The children thought I had robbed a bank.

The name of the club, which is now the dwelling of another company, shall not be named; to protect its patrons, employees, and professional reputation it once had.

I will say, however, defending this chosen field of work, my illusions of adult entertainment were slightly warped.

These young ladies, mostly single moms, use this dramatic approach in life to better their financial status.

Putting themselves through school, many that I had met moved along to prosperous employment. Med Star tech, Real Estate agent, teachers, one even became an attorney, just to name a few. Some even started their own businesses.

They were "not" into drugs, as we had random bag checks. All employees maintained a high level of professionalism and personal originality with their performance. Some presented problems. They made the way out the front door, as management always kept a tight reign.

Today, I hold no moral stand on this personal decision. Coming from the end of "the bra-burning era," "the battle of the sexes," and equal opportunity, I can Then something happened.

In all honesty, I can not judge. The refusal to elaborate on any events that took place is mine. The controversial issues and opinions of others prevent me from doing so. Acceptance is not an issue. The endless hours of cross debating, I have found to be irreverent and useless. It will be left spoken of as such. "Sometimes in life, you have to do what you have to do, to get where you want," something I always had said. I was happy.

FROM RAGS TO RICHES

So here I am, thirty-two years old, sober, working, going to meetings, stabilizing a once dysfunctional home life, and a new boyfriend.

Within a few weeks, we had new furniture for the living room, and a decent television set for the kids, a new dining table for eating our meals.

I also purchased a new bedroom suite for the children's bedroom. My son and daughter had "new" clothes, not used, thrift store items. However, I still, to this day, love thrift store shopping.

Funds were available for all of their school needs, plus money left over to buy them "real" toys. We had the money for proper medication if they got sick.

It was indeed a pleasure to at least have band-aids instead of using tissue and scotch tape. There was enough food to supply a whole army regiment.

Quite frankly, we were getting tired, watching other people eat on television. Now, they could eat in front of the TV and munch away. Life was getting better.

The children were at this time, spending every other weekend with their father. This helped tremendously, as "those" weekends; my time was spent working overtime.

I continued to go to meetings several times a week. The money was rationed as needed and saved to achieve the goal, to get off welfare, and to move to a suitable environment.

The children, especially my daughter, could not grasp the concept at the time why I was away most of the time. Looking back, I can relate to her feelings. The only objective in mind; stay sober, becoming financially stable, and being the best mother, knowing I was capable of being. Being home all of their life, I could understand how they must have felt, being gone quite a lot. I had no choice in the matter, except to listen. I knew one day they would understand my intentions. Single parenting takes a high level of expertise to juggle life in general.

When Jake brought the children home from his weekend visits, he was starting to inquire about the house. Noticing our newly acquired furniture and seeing that our lack of food was no more. All I told him was, "$30 a week, was not helping our children".

As I few weeks went by, money saved, plans were made for another suitable residence; I made a call to Social Services. You would have thought I was trying to get out of a complex business contract. If trying to succeed in getting into the public welfare system isn't difficult enough.

Successfully getting out is even worse.

They probed with questions, wanting answers "yesterday." My intentions of where I worked were interrogated. The competence of parenting was questioned. Also, my past drinking problems, of course, came up in the discussions. Before I knew, DSS and Child protective Services were knocking at my front door.

My disbelief, that "now," my accountability for providing a safe and secure environment for my family, was an issue.

The questions in my mind had arisen; 'where were you when the children were hungry"? "Where were you when my alcoholic behavior caused me to verbally and physically abuse them? "Where were you when we had no water, no electricity, and no home to live in"? "Also, "why" are you here now"?

The interrogation began in my living room. My sound explanation was; I am working, I am sober, as, for the children, you will find "no" signs of abuse nor neglect! They checked my refrigerator full of food. Their bedroom was inspected, tidy, clean, and organized. Remember, I was in the military. Everything was met for their expectations. My sobriety was brought up; one year and a half, then, of course, my employment. Given much maximum effort to remain calm during this time, I kept my mouth shut.

Finally, without reservation, assertively told them, "What part of, I am self-reliant, do you not understand"? "I no longer need your services. However, thank you anyway." With that ending "my" conversation, asked them to let themselves out of my home politely.

After they had left, I just sat there, on my couch, in disbelief.

I drank my coffee and finished packing for our new townhome. Understanding their concerns, my new self-confidence, and my sincere ambition to maintain harmony, remained unchanged. All the momentum was at this time, strengthen my family unit. It took a brief time to break away from the system. However, that was achieved.

THE PROBLEM CHILD

The day we moved gave us a new perspective on life. The determination to overcome adversity had been accomplished. I was happy. Most of all, the children finally had stability and happiness in their lives.

The relationship with my boyfriend was becoming serious at the time. Therefore, I asked him to reside with us.

This idea did not sit too well with my daughter. My son was jealous. I wanted to give my undivided attention to all. It was difficult to manage my time for everyone. My intense involvement in meetings, relations with my kids, work, maintaining household chores, paying bills, and Scott, my boyfriend, made me a significant driving force, as well as; tired.

The new adjustment seemed to cause behavior modification in the children.

My daughter displayed an intense desire for independence. Of course, she was 14 years old. She consistently questioned my lack of presence around the house. Knowing she could not possibly understand my commitments and responsibilities, I could never begin the express why. Our brief conversations always ended up in an argument.

I believe she hated me. My daughter never knew that afterward, I cried silently in my bedroom. She continued to barricade herself in her bedroom, the first one she ever had. Her grades were maintaining excellence, as always.

She never got in any trouble.

Except for when the park police brought them home one day, for trying to set the local field on fire, she was a good kid. Therefore, I left my teenage girl alone, giving her room to grow as an individual. She had earned it.

My son, 12 at the time, was starting to show signs of rebellion.

His attitude towards me was becoming belligerent. When he didn't receive what he wanted, nor couldn't do certain activities, the ability to maintain his anger became uncontrollable. In violent fits of rage, bashing his head repeatedly against any given solid structure was his taken action. He could not maturely handle disappointments. His compulsive behavior and inability to concentrate on any given task gave me deep concern. The consideration of the dysfunctional home life, they had up until now had come to mind.

I made the decision to take him to counsel. Therefore, contacts were made, and appointments set in action. It was at this time, and our lives were about to change.

THE KIDNAPPING

Jake had picked up the children on a Friday. I had worked two double shifts, as it was possible to do so.

Normally, with the kids there, 7 hours would have been the minimum. That Sunday, I was looking forward to spending some time with the kids, before Monday, as they had school. They were to arrive back around 3:00 pm. The time was now 5:00 pm, no, Jake. 6:30 pm, no, Jake, no kids. I continued to wait patiently and occupied my time with household chores. It was getting dark, looking up at the time; it was going on 7:00 pm. Now, there was a need for concern and worry. Upon numerous attempts, and no answer, I finally got through. I was relieved. Inquiring about the whereabouts of the children was my only thought. He told me, "I am not bringing them home, and there is an ex-parte against me from seeing them," and hung up.

My mind exploded with confusion. I had done "nothing wrong,"; I thought to myself. On my behalf, the authorities were called, and the investigation began. Seems, he had stashed them at his mother's house, upon waiting for an emergency change of custody trial. Horrible accusations against my boyfriend, and my incompetence as a mother were the reasons. This was unbelievable. What was the objective in his mind to make such a haste decision, of stealing my children away from their home? Trying to rationalize this, I could not. Looking back, if any thoughts of neglect or concern for his children's wellbeing, he could have informed me first, instead of taking these extreme actions.

Knowing it my heart, this had to be a terrible misunderstanding; I tried to maintain self-control over my emotions. After this terrifying experience, hitting a meeting was a must.

After sharing with my friends, this tragic event that had taken place, I was able to remain somewhat calm about the situation at hand. That is until my mothering instinct surfaced. Waiting for almost a week for the hearing, I was allowed no contact with the kids. I did rest peacefully until I had answers. My ability to reason with this situation became critical. It made no sense at all. So, I waited, but not with patience. I did not drink.

THE BLOWN-UP LIE

The court date arrived. His whole family arrived at the courthouse. The discussion began. Well, now, I get it. You better believe it "was" a huge misunderstanding.

Jake had found out, through my daughter, I was an adult stage performer. Then an accusation was made towards Scott. My daughter stated to him that while she was in the bathroom, making use of personal time, he had stood there and watched her. I was accused of never been home, assuming I was out parting all night, being that I was a drunk stripper. "Ok," "let me concur to these statements," I said.

I was trying extremely hard to keep my composure. I had explained to the magistrate, I had been gainfully employed, and the children needed for nothing. My job was never discussed with my children; however, they knew what I did for a living. Secondly, I have maintained my sobriety for almost two years, by choice. Going out to "party" was not an option, with all of my responsibility at hand. I worked, went to meetings, and cared for my children because I was their mother.

Sometimes, I slept. As far as the response to the allegations with Scott, that truth "was" revealed.

In our townhome, there was one main bathroom upstairs. My bedroom, as well the upper hallway adjoined to it. One day when I wasn't home, Scott opened our bedroom door to use the restroom. My daughter, sitting on the toilet at the time, was startled. Scott froze in his tracks, not expecting anyone in there. It took him a few seconds to regain thought. He apologized, and then closed the door.

Recalling his reaction made sense.

His reaction to uncomfortable situations had always made him pause in thought–something that was just in his character.

She finally admitted that "maybe" it didn't happen quite the way she had told the story. My daughter explained; she just wanted to live with her father. Ok, some pieces were coming together. Therefore, another court date was set for a custody hearing.

The children were allowed to come back home; however, Scott could have no contact with them because "they" didn't want him to reside with us. Well, now my boyfriend has been taken from me, for no reason at all, just he wasn't liked. So he moved out.

With my heart heavy, and concern for the children's emotional stability, I wept in silence. My daughter continued to ignore our much-needed conversations.

My son, trying to work through his emotions, only manifested more outbreaks of anger, towards himself, his sister, and me. He was greatly angered and desired not to leave his home.

After all the positive results that had desperately been achieved, Jake finally "came back in the picture," was trying to play dad and take away everything I had worked for. With personal convictions and confidence, I was going "head to head" with my worst nightmare, losing my children. I knew in my heart, I "was" of sound mind, with my entire decision making. An attorney was hired.

A few weeks had passed, and the picture was becoming clear. My daughter finally began talking. She had told me; dad promised her car when she obtained her learner's permit, as well as many other promises of material gifts.

My daughter explained to me that; she has never really spent time with her father and wanted to get to know him.

It was perfectly clear to me now, what she was experiencing, but could not articulate until now. I finally understood it.

Heartbroken, that I would miss her. I agreed.

She was right. My daughter had every reason to be able to get "to know" her dad. My sarcastic reaction remained only in thought. Being that he had been absent and/or distant for seven years, this might serve a great purpose. She was 14 and had the rights. The decision was mine; however, my son stays with me. He refused to leave.

POINTING THE FINGER

The court date came. Jake's entire family was present. Dolly was present, my attorney and I were ready. The interrogation began.

Without sufficient evidence, the ex-parte was lifted off Scott, alright, no problem. My home life, suitable standards, still no problem.

I was even commended and honored for maintaining my sobriety.

After an hour, his attorney, as well as the magistrate, made me appear to look like a slimeball maggot. The slanderous remarks and degrading accusations to my reputation were inexcusable.

I wondered, "how these people sleep at night." Their inappropriate judgment caused me to lose it a few times.

Looking back, that was the intention.

My job was brought up numerous times within the court session. Even the magistrate questioned my motives. "Can't you get any other job"? She asked. Then later, I explained that my job and nothing to do with this. I was almost held in contempt. It was at that time, I stood up from my chair and exclaimed, "and then why the hell, does everyone keep bringing it up"! "You're not asking "the father" why he works construction"—everyone in that room, silenced for few seconds.

With their high levels of education and those stupid little diplomas on the wall, they knew that the truth was spoken.

The fact is, they were discriminating against me. It made them mad; I had the guts to say it. I was made to sit down. With everything being put on the table, Jake and I were able to express our feelings before the decision was made. My recollection of Jake's story is void. The recall of my feelings and conversation remains embedded in my heart.

With tears in my eyes, I painfully expressed my feelings towards my children, and how deep my love for them was, and always will be, until the day I die. My intentions to provide for my family as a single parent had been established.

The courageous effort for ongoing sobriety was a daily task that was being maintained. I had even expressed my feelings of agreement with my daughter; she "should" spend time with her dad.

However, I was adamant about my "son" and his desire to remain with me.

All viewpoints were considered.

There was a brief recess, and then everyone came back into the room.

We all stood up.

The magistrate spoke. She said a few words and then addressed me. She said, "I want you to understand this has nothing to do with what you have done or not done." "Simply the fact your daughter is of legal age to make this decision," that to me was clearly understood. She had even commended me for not being sober. She continued, "However, I do not want to separate the siblings." "Excuse the "***k," outta me"? I said to myself. I had to sit down. "This is what happens when you are responsible"? I thought. This is the world I become sober for? My son, now screaming and crying hysterical, made me flip out, and blackout. I could not believe with all my productive efforts, to bring my family back to normality, this event was taking place, right in front of my eyes, and could do nothing. God could really use you now!

THE SYSTEM FAILED ME

All I can remember after that were tears, mine, my daughter, and of course, my sons. I felt like I had let him down profoundly, no way he could understand that the law is set in stone. The next event I remember was yelling in the hallway, and tears, and my son.

He was lying on the courtroom floor, hysterically crying. I ferociously looked at Jake and said, "You want to be a father, pick your son up, and hold him; he is hurting"! My reason for living had just ripped my heart to shreds. They only emotion other than hurt was pure hatred.

I remember going to a meeting that night. I did not drink. I remember nothing else, except feelings of anger, distrust in people, and hatred.

My love for my children remained in my heart. I thought of God.

UNFAIR JUSTICE

That night sleep remains unclear in my thought. The following day, the despair cost me absence from work.

My enthusiasm for life that had been recently acquired was painstakingly ripped from my heart. The visions for my family to be happy once more, crushed.

The pain of not having my children in my life made my soul build feelings of hatred; towards Jake, his family, and the entire judicial system. The anger that was felt made me violently bash my head into the kitchen floor, that morning. There was no rational explanation of why the two had to be separated. I had a clear understanding and accepted my daughters' motives. My son, especially, at this time in his life, needed his mother desperately. He had started counseling, and numerous appointments set, to be checked for ADD, and another psychological testing. I had shown my concern for him to continue with his therapy, his father, had a different opinion in this matter.

Jake had stated in the courtroom, "there is nothing wrong with him. He just needed a good family that sits down at the dinner table together".

With all the confusion going on, even "that" statement seemed idiotic. The magistrate had also agreed that the importance of ongoing counseling was in my sons' best interest. Therefore, it was ordered for him to continue. He never did.

Then to my surprise, the following day, Jake showed up at my front door. He had arrived in a small truck. I unwillingly opened the door.

Standing there with a stupid grin on his face, he said, "I came to get the kids things." "Excuse me,"?

I screamed. "What do you mean their "things." He wanted their bed, all of their clothes, toys, and school supplies.

I allowed the children to get clothes and school supplies and a few personal belongings they desired. No way, in God's creation, was this individual going to clean my blind, from all of the possessions that I worked hard for. He was forced to attain the proper items, for providing a suitable home for his children. This is what he wanted. This is every parent's responsibility to provide for their family. I clearly, directly stated to him, "be careful what you wish for." "Now, get the "hell" off my property," as I shut the door in his face. Then, I yelled out the window, "I will see my children in two weeks."

DENIED VISITATION

For those two agonizing weeks, I found a deep personal strength that was never before seen.

Sobriety had taught me acceptance, and my desire to drink was no more. Therefore, each day I totally absorbed myself with my job and my meetings.

My ability to rise beyond obstacles in life trials started to project e natural leadership persona at work.

Being that I was the oldest performer, that was almost expected from me. At meetings, this time, there was "always" something to share.

Many tears were shed, but they were my support system. My life had been destroyed once again. But somehow, to others, my radiance to shine, did not suffer.

The pain in my heart remained in hiding.

The intense anger in my spirit capitalized with extraordinary stage performance. For a woman of 32, that being well "over" the retirement age for this field. I rocked!

Still, to this day, I don't know if it was the professional expertise that was embedded in me as a child, or it was pain that had driven me. Guess, it really doesn't matter, it worked effectively. The money was being saved for my first "real" car, so I could see my children.

Two weeks passed, the time had slowed, but the day had arrived. Jake was called, and I had asked for him to provide transportation.

My vehicle was not in my possession as of yet. He refused, stating if I couldn't pick them up, not his problem. He then hung up the phone. Calling back numerous times, he refused my calls. That was a very long night. The next morning, the attempt was given again. I explained that transportation was being offered from Scott.

He again refused and hung up again.

Calling back several hours, he explained he wasn't allowed around the children. The matter had to be taken to court because the previous allegations against Scott had been settled.

THE TRUTH COMES OUT, GREED

I had to file an order for visitation, and it seemed like Jake had plans for action too. One week later, three weeks without seeing the children, my mail arrived at the house.

I opened a letter addressed from the courthouse. They must have set a date for trial. I am sure it was "a Kodak moment." I was being sued, from Jake, for child support. Now, without reservation, my understanding of the motive behind his actions was perfectly clear. It was about "money."

Our daughter was residing with his grandmother, and my son remained at his house with him. They had been "separated" after all.

That was not the decision made in court.

From my precise recall, this reason was "why" my son's desire to remain with me, was rejected.

He had shrugged off his parental responsibilities towards his daughter, and the promises he made, now is his desire to support "him," made it finalize his intentions. "The truth shall set you free." This is factual, in my opinion, because when we had nothing, he was not to be seen. When I needed clothes, financial help, groceries, and emotional support for our children, he had refused numerous times. I got it. These horrific events all took place because of my employment. The discrimination from Jake, his parents, and the "judicial system," left me with feelings of betrayal. I kept my faith. I did not drink.

The court date arrived. The atmosphere in the courtroom was mostly that of arguing. Jake was "slapped on the hand," for denying me visitation, and told not to repeat his mistakes. Child support issues were settled. It was apparent by my misconduct; the outrages amount was in just, to say the least. My need to work more than expected had to maintain consistency. However, I had always displayed loyalty to my employer and was granted extra hours.

I talked Jake into bringing the children to my house. That weekend was very awkward for all of us.

There was conflict.

In my opinion, they were being brainwashed to resent me.

Looking back, my prediction was correct.

However so, it is only an opinion. My daughter showing signs of great anger directed towards me, left our conversations brief, and time spent together distant. My sons' compulsive and violent behavior had worsened. The desire for him to come back home was so strong, and he could not successfully establish a pattern thought of how he felt. He only had the capably to express himself through anger. He destroyed everything in his room, which paved a small place for me to come in and talk with him. Calming him down, I brushed the tears from his face and mine.

Recognizing the immense pain we both shared, I told him, "Don't cry anymore, be strong as you can, and pray."

After the inevitable reality, they had to leave. I could not watch this. Tears poured from my eyes. The decision was made. The situation at hand is changeable, not acceptable. I will fight back for my son. It did not matter what the majority ruled, his best interest, was at home, with me.

I prayed for God's help.

THE BATTLE BEGINS

Scott and I had long conversations. Knowing that my reputation as an exotic dancer was playing a major role in decisions that were made, the work to regain custody was going to difficult. The discrimination was silenced, however, I knew, as did a lot of individuals.

Establishing a credible lifestyle in the eyes of the system was the target. It was a shame that proving myself, once again, at the only time period of my life that was indeed stabilized.

Scott supported my decision. Managing my finances strategically, I achieved my goal and bought a car. It was used 1992 Ford Mustang convertible.

A person would have thought the keys were handed to a Lamborghini. I could not wait to ride the children around town, top-down, and wind blowing in our hair.

I was so excited; breathing was an option. Then the reality hit. Jake still denied visitation. Legal action was taken again. The established court date took one month. The longing to be with my children and could not left me greatly sorrowed. The pain was, at times, unbearable.

The pleasant memories when we first moved into our house had vanished. My strong effort to endure the children's lack of presence made my decision to move.

It has been months now, going against repeated attempts of visitation denial, and only told, "stopping denying visitation." Needless to say, it persisted for almost a year: bogus reasons, every time. Exceptional knowledge, how the system worked, I represented myself in court after a while.

There are too many terrible situations that I am considerate to overlook. But, I must share my feelings with some. There were many times, especially with my son, even phone contact was almost impossible.

The calls that were "allowed" to take place were none respectfully monitored.

Not by Jake, but his girlfriend.

It was her house he resided in.

She was twenty years older than Jake, who makes sense, mother figure; he needed a knowledgeable woman to help him with decision making. Once I had called; my son was apprehension with the conversation, I asked if she was standing over him; He said, "Yep." Five minutes into the conversation, she ripped the phone from his hand and said, "you're finished talking to your mom," and hung up.

There were times when she refused to let me talk to him. It was not until, again, it was court-ordered, for her to "Butt out."

Jake hardly ever showed up for the hearings, only herself. She was finally condoned for taking his responsibility. One of the last days she was permitted to talk on his behalf, she came up to me and said, "I have your husband, I have your children, and now I have your money."

At that time, the fact is was dealing with a psychologically impaired individual deemed it necessary to bring my son back home, by all means necessary. By the way, I told her to keep my husband.

There was, of course, one Mother's Day, that was especially uneventful to forget. A Sunday, after not seeing the children for at least four months, Jake saw it in his heart to allow them time with me. It was not my visitation weekend. I had driven almost 100 miles, round trip, to spend Mother's Day with my kids.

It was great!

We ate at McDonald's and talked, and then I took them back to their Dad's. He never knew how much I appreciated what he had done for me. The whole "10 minutes" he allowed, goes well "beyond words." I cannot express how "that" felt, let alone the children's feelings. Do you believe in karma?

Looking back, sincerely, even those ten minutes meant the world to me.

I was happy.

The longest time period of visitation denial, was nine months.

Every time inexcusable reasons were given, and every time he was told to stop ignoring the court order for visitation.

The ongoing rejection of obeying the law persisted for years. This meant continuance effort on my behalf, to uphold the law, my rights, from their decisions. It took years. I am elated to see how well my judicial system worked for the best interest of my children. It was also my delight that our daughter was finally getting to know her father, even if the two weeks she lived with him was brief.

It was now, my passion of anger and resentment, over the decision my daughter had made, and everyone who helped promote it happen. I was not happy at all. The drama needed to end. I was indeed on a mission.

THE TEENAGERS

Scott and I remained together in our new apartment. Life, two years into the custody battle, was becoming tolerable to accept. My daughter is now a blossoming 16-year-old, my son 14. For my daughters' birthday, my mother invited us to her beach house.

She had picked the children up and brought them there. Jake was still controlling visitation rights. It wasn't "my" weekend, but mom saw to it that I was there. I drove my convertible. This special weekend will be cherished forever.

The personal desire to make her 16th birthday memorable was the highest agenda.

With great enthusiasm, I awoke early that morning. Wanting to buy her some beautiful long stem roses for the occasion was a must. That early, one store was found open. Of course, the only bouquets of red roses they had, the stems were wilting, and a few petals were falling off. I had to buy the that was all there was. Wanting to make the start of her day special, we all drove to the beach, 5 minutes away. Her anticipated reaction to the sunset rises up from the water that was going to be taped with my new camcorder. It started pouring down raining, of course, no sunrise. Besides, the battery for my camcorder had been left at the beach house.

When we got back, as time allowed me, while she was primping herself for the day, in the bathroom.

I beautifully arranged her flowers, beside her bed.

She gasped with delight and surprise.

As she picked them up to smell, every single rosebud snapped and fell to the ground. My son and I hysterically dropped to the floor, holding our stomachs, tears flowing, because we were laughing so hard. You see, the only way I could prevent the rosebuds from falling was to super-glue them to the stem. My son quickly helped me do so, previously before her entrance back into the room. We never said a word. That memory is priceless. My daughter was angry with our reaction to the incident. I didn't have the heart to tell her, knowing one day, she would understand my intentions to make her birthday special. It was for me and also my son.

THE 3RD MARRIAGE

As the summer past away, the year 2000, was directly approaching. The anticipation of the "computer crash" was expected.

It was exclaimed that "the end of the world" was coming soon.

Needless to say, with me, that event had taken place years before that predication.

Scott and I remained cohabited.

Our luxury high rise apartment, with my sate-of-the-art perfection for design, was kept at a high standard of excellence. The showroom quality appearance was professionally created.

The appearance would have put Macy's windows in New York City, to shame. My weekly, white-glove inspection made this possible.

We had gone on many weekend trips to local amusement parks. Having been to both Disney parks, California and Florida, made these entertainment spots look like carnivals, in hometowns, that were set up overnight.

However, the need to release the pressure of unnecessary confrontations with Jake and the court system made this an outlet for me to do so.

There was something about screaming wildly on a roller coaster, corn dogs, and eating cotton candy that made my life, at least, "bearable." Hours on end, I had fun. Looking back, our conversations remained to discuss the children and wishing they were there with us. As I was glowing with excitement, deep down, my thoughts were only of them.

Constantly, considering new tactics, to bring my son home, was my only reason to live, at this time. Forgiving Jake, my daughter's desire to keep distance between us and Jake's family's interference had become impossible to produce. My cold heart had become stone.

That New Year's Eve, we all took a trip to Atlantic City to engage in the festivities. It was an awesome event. The temperature by the beach, extremely cold, gave us the chance to ride the "people pulled" buggies around the boardwalk vicinity. Of course, that weekend, too, came to an end.

It was months before I was to see them again.

THE VEGAS WEDDING

The winter was long; spring was drawing near. In April, Scott and I flew to Los Vegas to be married. We exchanged our wedding vows at; "The Little Chapel of Flowers."

One woman there had taken me into a huge room, surrounded by dresses. She said, "take your pick," your choice is included with your wedding package. I chose a $10,000 white wedding gown, scattered with white pearls, which draped on the floor 12 feet behind me. I cried before I made my appearance back to Scott. Actually, the tears had been created, because my inability of resourcefulness lacked, to find a way to get "that" dress on the plane transport back home.

I was going to sell it to help pay child support. That was a "sarcastic" joke.

Our week's stay at Mandalay Bay was awesome. Real gold dust embedded the outer glass building. The room, gigantic in size, was delightfully decorated with an array of beautiful colors. Upon entering the huge bathroom, pure shock stopped me from even blinking an eye.

Scott and I remained still at the doorway, with a loss for words. Our now red hands, due to lack of circulation, because we had held them together for too long, responding to the overwhelming feelings, released themselves.

Have you ever seen a grown man cry?

The bathroom had a flawless white marble floor. All fixtures were made of gold. Two gold sinks adjoined together, on an exceptionally large, white, streaked gold counter made of marble. The gold sunken whirlpool spa, surrounded with gold faucets, ample space for displaying hundreds of white candles, was gigantic enough to fit eight people. In the corner was a separate gold shower with clear glass siding. Even the toilet was gold.

After observing the rooms, still crying from disbelief, yes, we did it. We jumped up and down on the bed, clothes on. Then hit the casinos.

This was my first "real" vacation since childhood, and I was in "Vegas" baby!

You know what they say; "what goes on in Vegas, stays in Vegas. My grief had been conformed to that of happiness, at least for one week.

My subconscious mind, to be with the children, still remained in thought.

Only wishing they had been with us, sharing the joy. I only wanted "girl- time" with my daughter when I was at the spa, wrapped with a white turban around my hair, thick white robe with matching slippers, after soaking in oiled waters. Envisioning her there beside me, sharing secrets, laughing, having time we had much deserved, made me so upset. Curling up to one of the dark green Italian marble fountains in the pool, tears were uncontrollably pouring from my eyes. Seeing this in my mind, I abruptly jumped out of the pool and vomited.

The reaction I had was never spoken of until now.

I became more depressed when Scott arrived back at the spa, two hours late; it was enough time to sulk immensely.

He was intoxicated; as I am sure he had to be, to explain to his new wife, he had just lost $4,000 at the crap table. The only thought had was, "I want to go home." My inability to speak to him during the last few days had made him, and I am sure, uncomfortable. That was a "long" flight home. It was days before the conversation between us resumed. God must have a sense of humor, I thought to myself.

We both regained recovery of our "Vegas" experience and proceeded with our lives once more. Everything that had occurred was forgiven and forgotten. As summer approached, visitation had become slightly regulated.

My son was nearing his 15th birthday and spending almost every other weekend with me. For the first time in many years, my happiness had been achieved.

We took advantage of the time and finally shared amusement park time together. We rode together, as we made Scott, the single rider. But, they were finally starting to bond. The summer was spectacular.

My 17-year-old daughter, at the time, remained distant. Spending her personal time, with her close circle of friends, was important for her. I understood. Therefore, I did not press the issue. She needed to seek her personal growth. Knowing she had high ethical standards, there was no concern to worry.

THE DAYTIME THIEF

One weekend, Scott, the children, and I spent a weekend at my mother's beach house. Needing to depart early, due to work, we drove separate vehicles.

It was fabulous.

Trust and bonding were starting to develop. My assumption was, at least.

Scott stayed one night and unfortunately left the following morning. The children and I continued our fun. We engaged in endless activities.

My mind at peace, giving me an enthusiastic spirit, the intense involvement with the children, made me extremely happy. Our feet sore, legs tired, from "too" much fun, we head towards a 5-star restaurant to reflect upon the moment. After a long day of activities and shopping, lobster and steak would be most gratifying.

The occasion was indeed special.

During the meal, my son proceeded across the room, tipping the piano player. When he did, the performer surprisingly boasted his head, atop the piano, and starred at our table. I assume he didn't receive many gestures of kindness. When my son arrived back at the table, I, being curious, asked, "how much money did you give him,"? His sister looked at him, they both giggled. Seeing that their dad had given them some spending money, I thought, well, "your" money to enjoy. I smiled and didn't pressure the intentions of goodwill.

Not recognizing they had acquired many frugal gifts also. The weekend ended with smiles.

A week later, Scott arrived at my place of employment. He had funds missing from his bank account, which could not be accounted for. After an investigation from the bank, it was traced to Ocean City. Evidently, my darling son, using no common sense at the time, watched Scott use his bank account pin and had swiped his card from his pants that evening prior to his leaving. Approximately $2,000 missing from the account was taken. Now, I had understood the incident at the restaurant.

Later on, finding out the information, that the piano player was handed a $100 bill, was why he reacted the way he did. We did not want to press charges against my son.

He made a terrible decision. The bank had no choice but to prosecute. Of course, when Jake found out, the blame was directed on me. The denial of visitation, until the set due date, again, one month without my children, was Jake's punishment.

Needless to say, the court drama was about to escalate.

LIES, LIES, AND MORE LIES

As phone contact, once again, was halted. Getting information from an outside source, I had connections that informed me of ongoing progress with my son. Jake never knew. Evidently, my son had been showing signs of rebellion towards Jake and his girlfriend.

Truancy in school had become a regular act of misconduct. Stealing was also a character trait he had also acquired.

Mild charges, misdemeanors, had been charged against my son.

His inappropriate behavior caused him to spend a few months in a boy's correctional facility.

This broke my heart. Then, I thought, when was Jake to inform "me," how my son's emotional instability was.

The anger and resentment directed towards Jake was growing immensely. Then, I realized something. I was coming up on three years sobriety. I went to a meeting. I knew in my heart, the challenges that had been created before me had a purpose.

That purpose was my focus to seek justice. To take everything being destroyed, give it to God, and use his strengths, a positive approach, and make it right again. My faith was growing.

The day in court, my son was released momentarily, to attend. I stated, to clear my name, had nothing to do with the disappearance of money from my husband's account. To verify this, I explained to the judge that engaging with the crime would be like stealing from "myself." Enough said, the judge agreed. My son's release had also been granted that day, from other charges. Jakes refusal to bring him home, because he and his girlfriend had plans for a vacation in Hawaii, left my son to reside back in the detention center, one week until they got back. The judge, considering my attempt to keep him, was denied. It was based on Jake's accusations of it not being in his best interest. I found out differently. My attorney had briefly stepped away during a break. Some papers were left beside me. Curiosity prompted me to look. One paper had a questioner that notably was "Jake's" handwriting. As I read silently, it was easy to understand the judges' decision.

Jake, on paper, desecrated my reputation.

He stated that I was a drug user, was an alcoholic, "still" drinking, a stripper, a neglectful mother with poor parenting skills, verbally and physically abused the kids, used cocaine, and smoked crack, and made Scott look like nothing short of a rapist. All extreme lies! When my attorney came back, I inquired about the findings. He said, "you don't really need to see that," and took the paper from my hands. I looked at him and said, "you really don't need to be employed"; "you're fired." My intelligent mind could not comprehend this "really" happened. I was thankful for my sobriety. At this time, so should Jake be also.

RUFUSING TO STOP FIGHTING

The pressure of court appearance numerous times a month, and the tragic events that surface was unbearable. My relationship with Scott, started to bring conflict and communication problems. Because now the fight for "custody" of my son was in the making, Scott knew I wouldn't give up. Therefore, acting as my own attorney, I researched data. My computer knowledge was complete illiteracy.

It took half an hour to turn it on.

Months prior to that, on a weekend visit, my son informed me we needed a new mouse. Wanting to please him, I proceeded to drive to "Pet Smart."

He lost bodily function, in the car, from laughing so hard, upon pulling up to the store. I felt like a moron, but his laughter cheered me up. Now I tell the story to others to lighten stressful situations. Looking back, it was indeed hilarious.

Another year passed.

My daughter's 18th birthday present was a trip to Disneyworld. Our relationship was beginning to show signs of reconnection. Still quite vulnerable, but an adult, I proceeded with caution.

With time, I knew all amends would be made. So, I waited on her prompt for communication. Her critical dedication to school gave her the benefits of a nursing scholarship. That made me so proud. Knowing she was finally of legal age, after four long years of debate, eased my mind, as far as "she" was concerned. Jake, at this time, was even restraining his efforts for visitation denial. My persistence of loyalty to my son never stopped.

Besides, in two years, "he" would be of legal age.

I was beginning to become grateful that the children got to know their father. As far as Jake's concern, my belief, he got more than what was expected from parenting. In my opinion also, from my numerous court fillings, he wishes he had never met me.

My life was becoming controllable, once again, from many years of anguish.

The passing of yet another year was upon us. Repeated denial of custody was delegated. It mattered no more. Less than a year, my son will be 18. The fight was over. My son had dropped out of school, minor incidences had occurred, but his stability was soon being prepared by myself. Scott and I had currently broken up. The desire to move closer to work was established. I had now been employed with the same employer for five years. As now I am 37. Fully prepared and well established with finances for a suitable dwelling, just like it was "five" years ago. However, everyone's perception of me was changed. The assumption I had was; they knew now; "no" was not in my vocabulary. Never to admit the fact; I believe Jake realized he made a terrible mistake.

MY NEW LOVE

My new home was "mine." With steady progress, I continued to construct my son's room for his homecoming at the end of the year. Quite a few months ahead gave me ample time to do so. Work kept my time occupied as well. I had started to date my friend, our DJ at the club.

We had known each other for many years and grew very fond of each other. Now, the time has come for the admittance of a secret.

Scott and I indeed got married in Los Vegas. We loved each other very much. Our road trips, vacations, and shared time together were wonderful. The marriage was a "stage effect." It was solely a tactic to demonstrate credibility for acquiring custody of my son.

The vows were exchanged two weeks prior to the custody hearing. However, it did not work as planned. This was the extreme measure that was forced upon me, to take. My intentions only had one direction; my son's desire to come home.

The unconditional love for him pushed me to extremes. I am grateful he did this for me. We parted as friends. However, it concluded with a messy divorce—the effort to elaborate ends with that statement.

A few painstaking months went by.

Work continued as usual, and my friendship with Brad developed into a love affair. We kept it a secret from work employees, as we were not allowed to fraternize with each other. They found out somehow, but we were accepted as a couple. He is 6'4", half Native American, and me 5'4", blonde, mostly of German ancestry, looked cute together to everyone.

Many nights, he came over for dinner and to watch movies. He introduced his two children, and we all seemed to develop a positive relationship together. Telling them about my sons returning home after he turned 18, excited them to meet him.

Since Brad, my new boyfriend, and I were starting to build a closer relationship, their reaction pleased me.

A few more months, my son was coming home. The feelings of excitement and concern gave me mixed emotions. I was ready, but scared. We had been separated from each other so long; the adjustment was going to be difficult. The ability to suffer as I had, as well as my son, and not drink, surpassed my understanding to this day. I was indeed sober. It had been almost six years since my last drink.

I had a special evening planned for Brad one Sunday. The dinner I prepared was spectacular. Homemade spaghetti, with freshly baked garlic bread, and enough salad for an army, he was impressed. Still stuffing his face, I had asked him to check out some movies on cable. We were having a blast, laughing; he was a great comedian. As I was cleaning up in the kitchen, the view to the living room was clear, because of the large oblong window sill connecting the two. My verbal expressions were given to him, that he and my son were going to get along because he had an imaginative sense of humor.

Brad was an exceptional single father and understood feelings, more than any man I knew. His mother was full-blooded Native American, making him half-bred maybe that was the reason for his sensitive nature.

THE DREADED KNOCK

Our pleasant evening had been interrupted, with an abrupt knock at the door. I paid no attention, as nothing was going to ruin this special evening that had been planned in advance, for weeks. I told Brad; pay no mind, they will surely go away.

The children in the neighborhood played pranks all the time. He jokingly agreed, raising two boys by himself. The knocking stopped. We continued talking, after 20 seconds, there was another knock at the door. This time it was a firm, repetition of knocks.

These sounds were all "too" familiar.

I knew now; this was not a child's playful gesture to get on my nerves, to disrupt my evening.

For certain, it was another attempt from Jake to serve me papers for "something" again.

That was a policeman's knock. I hesitantly walked down the hall towards the door. The thought of looking out the window was useless.

I just wanted to get it over with.

Displaying a readiness to accept the serving, I opened the door. There standing in front of me, my son. He ran in with excitement and said, "I'm home; let's eat."

For the next five minutes, I heard my son explain to Brad, how his father let him come home because he was almost 18.

They were sitting there laughing like they were old-time friends. I, for those five minutes, was still standing at the door, facing outside looking at my son. Ten minutes went by, still at the door, facing outside, looking at my son.

My physical body went into shock; they both had to pick me up to place me on the couch. I could not speak nor move. After 15 minutes or so, they had said; the ability to grasp the situation at hand made room to think clearly. I had my first out of body experience. This was impossible. Of course, the call had to be placed with his father, to verify his whereabouts. Sure enough, Jake could not take the pressure of parenting anymore; he released my son to me.

It was done. I was inconsolable. All of my hatred diminished. I remember nothing neither more of that evening with Brad or any conversations with my son. But I do remember that night. My son slept in my bed; the willingness to let go of him was not going happen, ever again.

For the first time in six years, we both slept the entire night. I had my reason to live. God released my "pain" because he released "my son."

Honestly, my recollection of the following weeks, are of no remembrance.

The event that took place apparently shocked my nervous system greatly enough, to wipe out all of my memories, and conversations with anyone. I can not even recall going to work. I loved God with all my heart.

A PERFECT LIFE

As fall approached, winter and the holidays were around the corner.

My recollections of events retain no memory. It was a brief time period, before my capacity to accept; that which had happened.

However, memories of Thanksgiving and Christmas remain in my heart.

As Brad, his two children, my son and I resided in one household: four males, one female. It was overwhelming at times, but we adjusted; as such. The first holiday, Thanksgiving, was great. We celebrated at home. My mother had been invited, as well as my daughter. The kitchen counter was filled with an abundance of vegetables, salad, and meats. A large ironing board was set up for the placement of deserts. The 20-pound turkey was incredibly moist. Picking it up with two large spoons, the whole turkey divided it two. The stuffing was placed in the middle of the bird, and I shoved it back together. No, I did "not" use crazy glue.

Everyone enjoyed themselves. The happiness that I felt was priceless.

Christmas quickly arrived thereafter. My son, at the time, was a diehard NASCAR fan. "Tony Steward" was his favorite driver. Needless to say, after Christmas, orange; was the only color that was visible in his room.

My agenda was to make the holiday season most memorable for everyone. Being in that spirit; to sum up; Brad and I between them both, spent close to $4,000. Details of gifts would be "too" many to mention. However, our families had a most memorable Christmas.

I had, other than my son's presence, received the best gift.

My daughter, with great enthusiasm, grabbed me by the arm Christmas Eve and pulled me aside.

She held her slender hand out and said nothing. Not knowing her intentions, glanced at her hand.

I was now looking at the biggest "rock" I had ever seen. With my mouth wide open, all I could do was "nod" my up and down, as she did the same.

I am sure the neighbors had heard my screams thereafter. Her boyfriend had proposed. My daughter was getting married. The joy I felt was indescribable. I was so happy that she wanted to share this special moment with me. My daughter never knew that sharing this, and wanting to be near me, meant; until now. At this time in my life, I was complete.

My son, now 18, desired not to spend time with his father. I had "no" comment.

THE IGGIE PROJECT

The following spring, Brad and his 13 years, my son and I drove to a pet store to buy food for our fish. I, being a lover of canines, had to check out cages in the back of the store to see the pups.

They were all adorable. One particularly was unusually beautiful.

The appearance was that of a Chihuahua. However, it had long slender legs and was grey in color. I knew my breeds of dogs, numerous researches with the encyclopedia as a child, gave me knowledge. This had to be a "cross-bred" of something.

After inquiring information from the salesclerk, I figured what this adorable little pup was. She was an Italian Greyhound. My assumption was a Greyhound from "Italy." Then she explained it was a "miniature" version of a Greyhound.

At this time, the family came over; to see what I was doing.

Pulling Brad by the arm, I said, "check this out." He cocked his head and scrunched his top lip to his nose and said, "what the hell is that."

Of course, by then, our intense observation with the dog got the attention of his son and mine.

They yelled out together, "can we get a dog"!

My son understood, but I said, "no," I am allergic to the dander." Still standing there, the clerk said, "this breed is hypoallergenic." Meaning, in short, does not carry the dander, which causes my allergic reaction.

Recognizing the opportunity to make a quick sale, she delicately pulled the pup out of the small cage. She insisted we play with her.

We all gathered together in a small enclosed play area for pets.

The IG was almost the size of a Chihuahua. She had "extremely" long legs, almost the same width of a cigarette.

Lack of confidence to hold her prevented me from doing so, as she appeared "so" fragile.

Brad and the boys played with her.

Of course, my family desperately pleaded to keep her. Their persistence with me remained until she was put back.

To establish calmness with the situation, to keep them quiet, I had no choice but to inquire. I thought, "here comes the sales pitch." The salesclerk was speaking in a pleasant tempo; "we have a 20% sale this week on all pets".

I had to stop her there. Explaining to her, we just came in to purchase fish food.

The kids were disappointed. She kept strategic persuasion. As a previous reservist in the army, I had worked at a psychological warfare unit.

I knew "all" the tactics.

Finally, I asked, "how much is she"?

She politely smiled; $1,120 before taxes". Everyone was disappointed because I just walked away, angrily mumbling, "no way, I was going to spend that much money on a dog"!

No one spoke to me "all" the way home. When we arrived back, the conversation began again. They knew my weaknesses. I had agreed to at least go back the next day to see if she was "still" for sale. My convictions of refusing to buy a $1,120 dog remained. No way. The intent was meant for my family's silence towards this poor decision.

Brad and I went back to the store. My course of action, with haste, was to satisfy them to at least show interest.

The same salesperson was there. I had explained to her in private, my intentions. She said, "awe, why you don't hold her." I shook my head. Brad approached as he was still in the "front" of the store.

He took the pup into the play area, I followed. He was radiating with joy, holding her. I am still refusing to buy her. I exclaimed to him again, "I am "not" spending over a thousand dollars for a dog." "No way,"! I said. She was dainty and adorable, however. But, I just couldn't do it. He said, "just hold her," I refused. He said it again; "just hold her," and gently, but forcibly laid the pup in my arms.

The acceptance to take her was inevitable because she would have dropped to the floor if I didn't.

Alright, she was cute, I had admitted.

The baby, IG's big beautiful hazy eyes glared right to mine. I gave him back; Brad was disappointed.

I told him to stay here at the store while I ran some errands.

I came back twenty minutes later. Placed down $1,120 on the counter and wrapped Mini-Me in the pink princess blanket, I had just bought for my new "baby." Brad cried. I had fallen in love with her at first sight, literally. That is why I could not hold her before. My heart knew. Their persuasion promoted my decision. Two months later, we put in a request for a "male" IG. He was tiny and weighed 4 pounds. We called him "Hercules." He was the "baby." For the record, we never got the fish food.

My love for the "Italian Greyhound" breed grew immensely. Mini-Me was a big girl for an IG. She weighed 16 pounds, which was overweight for the breed.

However, suitable for an "unexpected" litter of seven, she and Hercules produced. We had grandbabies three times. We determined that Hercules was a compulsive achiever; therefore, the need to have Mini-Me spaded, was necessary. I did, however, obtain a breeder license.

They have legally registered purebreds as; "Queen Catherine Victoria and Lord Achilles Ramses.

These individuals all owned Italian Greyhounds. My personal research gained knowledge, respect, and love toward IGs.

So much, that I designed the website for them, only being the "copy and paste" type.

However, the positive feedback from friends, persuading me to further my creativity, promoted a desire to investigate that possibility.

Those few years that had past were utterly wonderful. My daughter, well into nursing school, was visiting on a regular basis. She brought her laundry. I was just happy to see her. She and her brother were becoming closer than ever. They were always close, however now, they were inseparable. She always treated him with gifts and food from their "mall "trips. Her acts of kindness brought them closer together. My father used to say, "everything happens for a reason."

The outcome of the dysfunctional past was starting to reveal the meaning behind this message.

As wonderful bliss had blessed my home once more, this time for two years, I was happy. Then something happened.

THE FALL FROM THE CEILING

My son had been working with Brad. During the weekdays, he was a carpenter by trade. I received a phone call at work. My son conveyed that Brad fell through the roof, three floors unto the basement floor.

He was rushed to the hospital. My son encouraged me to get there immediately. Not knowing what to expect, I rushed to the hospital. He had been released almost as soon as I had arrived, 30 minutes later, with minor injuries.

I was relieved.

That night, and early the next morning, immense pain remained.

The medicine they gave him was insufficiently working. So he remained in bed.

A few hours later, the phone rang. It was Brad's hospital. Evidentially, with a closer observation of his X-ray, they found a small chip of bone resting on his spinal cord. The doctor insisted that he be flown to Washington Hospital Center for immediate surgery. We rushed him to the nearest hospital for transport.

It was explained in the emergency room, the procedure needed to be performed. This type of injury ran the risk of being paralyzed from the waist down, or worse, fatality. Up until now, my growth in dealing with the unexpected had matured. I will say that I broke down in tears. Brad remained calm and consoled me. My son's mature attitude to handle this crisis with composer surprised me. Their reactions strengthened me, and I regained control.

I remember the helicopter lifting off the ground, the enormous wind, and Brad's long legs hanging out the back of the chopper.

As he briskly flew away, I looked beside me at my son. I had to laugh. My only thought was, "someone had indeed put a curse on me." Then tears flowed again down my cheeks, my son and I prayed. I did not drink.

Brad had two surgeries done in a few months. One plutonium rod, with numerous screws set inside.

The recovery was long in progress, was very demanding on me for his care. But, he did have a full recovery, with minimal pain.

BAD LUCK OR CURSED?

Life continued, but with unneeded stress. His inability to productively function for those two months encouraged his son to misbehave towards my son and me. Looking back, I believe he just had feelings of concern for his father.

I had to work enormous hours; the accumulation of bills had become enormous. Back-child support was still being allocated to Jake every week. A recent family trip to Disney World, months before the accident, left me with five credits cards, severely overdue. While Brad waited for his workman's comp to be settled, my son worked part-time to help make ends meet. I was still working with the same employer.

Numerous arguments about money, the boys potentially volatile fighting, breeding IGs, work, maintenance of the house, and playing nurse to Brad were burning me out. The ability to balance my responsibility was declining.

Six months had passed, and Brad was capable of working weekends.

However, the damage had been done, and the relationship was deteriorating. With so much concentration on focusing on the rising problems, I had failed to seek solutions. Looking back, that was the reality. Brad and I truly cared for each other. But, the constant conflicts between his son and me, and my son with him, indeed had to stop. The only resolution would be to separate. My only desire at that time was to be with my son. I wanted harmony back in our lives. I had no energy nor a need for conflict in my life.

Focusing back on my son, my daughter, and my mother, I regained sanity once more. Brad and his son left, leaving me thousands of dollars in debt.

I was not too happy. Because at this time, I had recognized a potential for web design and was accepted into a very pristine school on-line. I started college at 42. My goal was to get my associate degree in web design. My acceptance letter had arrived two months before he left. Somehow, during this stressful time, I managed to keep a straight A-average. Of course, every time my grades were posted, I cried.

COLLEGE BOUND

Now, my son being almost 21 years of age and myself, resided together. My daughter 23, now "happily" married for three years. Her continuing effort for finishing nursing school is secure.

She and her husband are both employed with potential growth success within their fields of choice. My mother, 74 years young, still works part-time. After retiring, some years back. Lack of financial security not being the reason she got bored.

My son had been working several days a week. Giving much consideration for our current situation, I asked him to reside at home. To keep maintenance of our home, and responsibly to care for our "four Italian Greyhounds, he would be paid in return. This decision caused me to work extremely long enduring hours. He quickly grasped the new routines as a new learning opportunity. I was impressed with his ability to do so. This was the first time he had ever displayed responsible emotional maturity.

The week after Brad left, our electricity got turned off, due to an enormous unpaid bill. The accountably to resolve the issue, took one week. My school was informed and was granted an extension for assignments. Studying and working by candlelight until 4:00 am, for three days, earned me another A.

My son adjusted that week also.

Most nights anyway, he spent time with his newly acquired friends. He was 21 and needed his "own" time. I respected that, however, insisted on a curfew of 2:00 am.

Another month passed, more bills mounted, and my son became less responsible for his delegated duties. We had many discussions and came to terms with many issues at hand. He was bored and wanted to go back to school to obtain his GED. That was pleasant to hear, therefore, fully supported his decision. We made arrangements. He enrolled and gave much effort to do so. The desire to work, earning his own money was expressed to me. I agreed.

We both now had a personal commitment to our lives. With our separate ambitions and challenges, we worked together to achieve our goals. I was nine years sober, working, going to school, and praying. Then something happened.

TESTING NEW WATERS

One evening, after a long day's work, my son was at home, upon arrival. He had missed school and did not go to work. My assumption, due to illness, had remained home for the day.

With concern for his health, he approached and sat down beside me. Before the conversation had begun, I knew. His eyes were red and glazed, and when he spoke, it was slightly impaired. The familiar smell of alcohol jolted my senses, making me almost vomit. The weed aroma was apparent as well. My son was stoned and intoxicated. This was unacceptable behavior to me.

Knowing that confronting this issue was impossible at the time, it had to wait until morning. We had a long conversation. My reasoning and concerted attempt for his understanding of alcohol and drug abuse left him in remorse. We closed the incident with amends. He promised "never" to make that mistake again. I let it go.

Life resumed as always. Three days later, arriving home from work, my son, the same couch, intoxicated. We again had another conversation the next morning. This time, trying to be broad-minded, but "reminding" him of my difficult recovery process with alcoholism. Expressing my love and concern for his well being, he had understood my anger for his irresponsible actions. This time, in tears, he exclaimed, "I will never do it again, I swear Mom"! I forgave him, and walked upstairs to my room, to silently cry. My only thoughts being at the time; "prayer", I prayed for him and myself.

THE JOKESTER

The next few weeks had been difficult financially. My son had learned a valuable lesson and regained his natural comedic, energized originality, that was a character trait of his. I was relieved. One morning, studying downstairs at the computer table, leaning back, on my over-sized swivel rocker, I flipped backwards and hit the floor. My legs sticking straight up in the air, made me unable to move. Making breakfast in the kitchen, my son was laughing deliriously. I thought, "okay, no problem". He and I always played practical jokes on each other. This was an accident; however, he denied my accusation, and I believed him. Though, my sense of humor gave thought to a plan of action for a joke, seeing he thought "this" was "so funny to him.

He was anticipating my response for revenge, so I wait for sufficient time to plan for action. A week later, working an extremely long day, I sat down in my favorite dining room chair when I arrived home. After I sigh of relief, I stretched my tired arms out and clasped them together, putting them behind my neck for support. Took a long yawn and looked up. Discovering, numerous household items that had been strategically tacked to the ceiling, left me speechless. My son, softly giggling upstairs, was the culprit. On my ceiling was a pack of cigarettes, a small stuffed animal, plastic Tupperware bowls, assorted paperwork, jewelry, an old doll of my daughters, and an inverted plastic soda bottle. As I sat there staring in amazement, my only thought was, "how the hell, he got the tack in the bottle. I had to laugh. When he came down, I commended his innovative creativity for this idea. We laughed together. He refused to give knowledgeable insight into the bottle "trick".

But I persisted; he had ample time to explain, given the "responsibly" to take down every single item. He never revealed his secret to me. Standing there laughing, I thought, "I am going to" bring" him down". This was hard to top, however.

A few days had passed, a morning resumed as usual. My son asked to use the computer that morning. Preparing breakfast, reluctantly permitted until I finished some chores. We had designated times for usage of the computer, as we had just one. He enjoyed his games. I took two steps to the right to watch. Jumping into the large swivel chair, he pushed his body back to relax.

The chair abruptly collapsed into several pieces, like a tall building being destroyed with explosives. In shock, unhurt, he remained unmovable, except for a slight turn of the head towards me. Standing there with no expression on my face whatsoever, nodded my head up once, and then grinned devilishly.

The night before, I waited until he was asleep. I went downstairs, with a screwdriver and loosened every screw holding it together.

"He" was impressed. Laughter at the expense of each other remained ongoing and priceless. Never admitting; "he was the master". I managed to keep "crazy glue" out of his possession.

Everything in life, even the enormous pressure of "past due" notices received in the mail, seemed functionally improving. It was shortly after that, my life was about to change unexpectedly.

ALL TOO FAMILIAR

My son and I were frequently bickering over nonessential issues. Rare occasions led to brief arguments. Losing interest in school, as well as work, concerned me. His newly acquired friends were his priority. Failing to obey the curfew that was set, a confrontation was necessary. Upon our interaction together, he confided in me that he had been parting. Of course, "he didn't have to explain, I already knew".

He told me, "don't worry, I have it under control". Over the next few weeks, my numerous attempts to intercede his actions failed. Once again, in tears, I confronted him. As he stood there screaming in my face, he said, "I have it under control"! Then he slammed my bedroom door, before the entrance to his, and remained silent.

Sitting on my bed in utter shock, with tears pouring down my face, finally understood. At that instant, I realized why we always had an inseparable connection. Analyzing his motives of thought and action throughout his life came to mind. Then I knew. My son had always projected the character traits of a terrible disease.

That of which is called; "alcoholism".

My world shattered to pieces. The thoughts that were had gave me unbearable pain. I prayed to God for help.

THE SUICIDAL CHILD

I maintained a distance from my son, my sobriety, and emotional stability had become threatened. Having being counseled this approach, from others with more experience. My job, requiring high energy and enthusiasm, made my appearance at work seem uninfluenced with events in my personal life. One day, working at the admittance register, a gentleman said, "you sure look happy, what is your secret". If he only knew, my heart was breaking in two". Thanks were given, he went inside, then I thought, "sobriety". I smiled.

When I arrived home, my son was out.

He had been residing at the computer, upon looking, my stomach almost busted from its skin. "1001 ways to die", was the site. Frantically calling all area hospitals, inquiring his whereabouts, is my only "recollection" of this event. However, the chain of events to happen, "this" was just the beginning.

As his alcohol and drug use escalated, the belligerence towards me, and uncontrollable anger began to escalate most frequently. His sister was the only person who could reach him. With her interceding regularly, it helped for the period allowed. She had always been a positive influence in his life, even when they were separated, the admiration and respect remained. I trusted her motives for influence. However, many attempts led to disastrous results. To see him like this broke "her" heart too.

My son now was displaying acts of self-inflicted knife cuts to his chest and upper arms. His use of alcohol/drugs were now daily abusive rituals.

The overwhelming emotions had almost placed me in the hospital, upon receiving a phone call from work; from the state police. Rushing to the location, that was informed to me, was my son. He had laid out flat on the highway, wanting to be run over. The policeman acted accordingly, asked if he used drugs. I assured the officer, he will get help. The next day I went to a meeting. I took my son.

The day after, I received a phone call at work. It was the local police; my son was admitted to the hospital. Explaining, he had climbed a water tower, holding a knife, with threats to kill himself—there where no injuries, they were holding him for physiological evaluation. The unit, holding his hands in restraints, was needed for his safety. I refused to visit, for seeing this image in my mind, would surely contribute a factor for thoughts of suicide for myself. The only "sanity" I had was sobriety. He remained there for one week.

Upon his arrival back home, I was dedicated to understanding and acceptance of his behavior. But with gentleness, insisted he attend meetings with me, and seek physiological counseling. He agreed. We both cried and forgave.

Another work week passed. I arrived home as usual. The television was on in the living room. My son and I started conversations of our day. The instant he spoke, it was apparent. After 5 seconds, his slurred speak and inability to keep his head from moving, I knew he was intoxicated. My display of anger was now uncontrollable. Reacting to my response, he reacted with violence. When he got up, the realization of his high level of intoxication was verbally and physically expressed. His severe rage led to several holes being punched in the wall.

It finally escalated to him, pulling a knife on me. Through the confusion, I still understood, made my decision, and called the police.

They arrived swiftly and took him away.

My intentions were sound and clear.

I wanted to intentionally make me son, "hit his bottom", before this disease did. Reflecting back, it was never in my control. I can not recall it after that.

CO DEPENDENCY TRIALS

Awaiting his trial date, gave time to reflect. My terrifying thoughts haunted my dreams every night, consequences of his actions.

The recollection of any other events is void, at this time in my life. We went to court. I dropped the charges he was accused of. After seeing him in handcuffs, the desire to help him was now my only reason for living.

I expressed to the judge my feelings.

He was released. My son came home.

For the next weeks, my walk on eggshells remained. All my nervous energy was engulfed with work, school. My son accompanied me to many meetings. This meant the world to me. He was remaining sober and not misbehaving. This made me extremely happy. My personal prayer life was ascending to a new spiritual level as I cried every night for acceptance, forgiveness, and asking in prayer for God to use my life for his purpose and will.

For two weeks after that, my prayers had been answered. The splendor bliss that was felt in the household was becoming our "new" reality. His self-respect was developing once more. He and my daughter regained companionship and trust again. School resumed as always, with straight As.

Yes, there is most definitely a God, and he loves me. It is now fall, the middle of October, the year 2006. An event is to happen to change our lives forever.

THE WORST NIGHTMARE

I worked that whole day, with exceptional enthusiasm and was highly energized to prepare dinner. My charisma at work had increased dramatically as a result of the gratifying home life I was living. I was becoming economically viable once again. The ongoing strategic plans of organizing a well-balanced system to resolve debt issues were successfully working. Hours beforehand, I had asked my son to defrost the chicken for dinner. He insisted on grilling himself, I, of course, agreed. With his exceptional creative ability, especially with cooking, the day was ending with a great victory. Being touched by his kindness, I wanted to surprise him with a dessert, "cheesecake; which was his favorite.

Unanticipated chores at work detained me an extra half hour. I called home, no answer, therefore; left message on the machine, explaining my lateness, and apologized for being late. The cheesecake was never mentioned. With much resentment towards my employer, I was finally able to leave.

My departure from work made me almost an hour late for dinner. I stopped at the store, got the cheesecake, and headed home.

We lived in a townhouse development that was safe and well maintained. The only time police were present was at our house. They responded numerous times each week, due to my son's previous actions of misconduct, and suicidal behavior attempts. The fire department and ambulatory services that had arrived with them were also seen.

Two streets down, driving up the winding embankment, made the right-hand turn towards the house. I was so excited, finally to eat dinner, by this time I had become famished. It was dark, but the "sky" was illuminating brightly. There were hundreds of lights circling repetitiously around the neighbor's townhomes and glancing to my left, the end unit, my house, with all the inside lights on.

Approaching closer, my backyard, in plain view, were eight police officers. There was no room for parking. There were two fire trucks and several ambulances in front of "my" house.

My worst nightmares could not remotely come close for what was to come. My stomach resided in my feet, with trembling in my body, hesitantly parked and got out.

The whole county police force knew me by now. As I walked towards my door, two police officers approached me; in my disorientation, it appeared as a surreal slow-motion walk. I passed the back yard, smoke-filled my back-door entrance.

My reasoning led me to believe, my son accidentally caught the house on fire. As the police were now standing in front of me, their look of concern gave me a reaction of denial. One officer extending his arm out; said, "Madam" I stopped him right there.

Stating, "Don't you dare tell me".

The denial that something happened to my son was firmly ingrained inside. They insisted on speaking as I walked away to greet my son. The other police officer gently grabbed my arm to stop me. "Madam"; there's been a horrible accident. Confused and disoriented, my mind didn't comprehend what they were trying to tell me.

They were trying to relate to me the incident that had happened. Still, in a haze, the conversation was paused, with the overhead blaring motors and chopper blades of a Med Star helicopter. They explained; your son is with them. Extremely relieved that he was indeed alive, I could breathe. Then they proceeded to tell me. That while grilling outside, he had taken gasoline, they were told, poured it on him, and had set himself on fire. My reaction left me paralyzed with any emotion.

One officer had said, seeming been traumatically affected by the incident; "it was the worst thing he had ever seen". He had described that his flesh was peeling off his bones.

They told me, leave immediately to Washington Hospital Center, as it looked like he was not going to survive this ordeal. I could not cry; I could not "feel anything". But I knew in my heart; if my son died, my suicidal attempt would be spent in eternal damnation. I could not "live" without my son. God was looking pretty evil right now to me. My life is given to you, and in return, you want to kill my son, I thought to myself.

Still shaking, still horrified, drove to the hospital. I had called my mother. It only took approximately 20 minutes for the 40-mile drive, as my speed limit excelled close to 92mph. I ran every light, crossed over yellow lines, and went right through stop signs. One homeless woman was almost struck by the car.

I had no concern about looking back.

I cursed God and blamed everything that was happening. The need for Jake's appearance was only to punch him in the mouth. I never wanted contact with my daughter ever again. My hatred, blame, and resentments escalated every second before my arrival.

THE BURN UNIT

Before realizing it, I was at my destination and cannot recall parking my vehicle. My only recollection was screaming in search of him. The assumption was my guidance had been directed.

Getting lost numerous times, I had found the right floor, and burn unit. Walking at a fast pace, down the 45-mile long hall, two doctors approached, pushing a hospital bed, a large man resting on top. His large black head protruded from the sheets. I knew I was close to the burn unit.

When they passed, I slowly glanced back with compassion. I then noticed strands of red hair protruding from his head, the same color as my son's hair.

I thought to myself; this man is not my son. My strong knowledge of the unique color, I ran back and inquired. They confirmed to me he was my son. Rushing me into the elevator, they exclaimed, "come on; we got to go now!"

In the elevator, one doctor explained the desperate procedures necessary to save his life. Hearing the information, everything he was saying had been a fragment of whispers through a straw, as my attention was focused on my son.

I, in denial that this was happening, I remained calm. The ability to grasp the idea; this was my "son" could not be reached. My son is 5'5', and 140lbs soaking wet. This 300-pound man was "accidently" confused with another person flown in from Med Star. Looking, standing beside him briefly, I then felt nothing.

The door opened, rushing him away down the hall, one yelled, "Call everyone in his immediate family".

Stating it was indeed a great chance, he was not going to survive. I am now standing in the 12 by 12 corridor entrance to the elevators. I was rushing around in a circle, getting lost; I felt a cinderblock being smashed to my chest. The excruciating pain was indescribable. No conceivable pain in "hell" could compare to what I just experienced. The reality was apparent. As my body collapsed on the floor, my knees prevented the fall. I must have mentally blacked out because I found myself curled up to the floor windowsill, moments later. I wept to God and prayed to spare his life. I even bargained with him, to somehow miraculously switch our bodies, and allow me to die for him. As I prayed, I envisioned my life without him. Peace started to arise in me, knowing that if he died, I would go with him.

With that thought, I got up and called everyone in the family. The thought of explaining to his sister the urgent rush to arrive at the hospital, fear overcame me. Knowing she might be incapable of driving. My conversation cannot be recalled. Dolly arrived shortly before her, the absence of memory, I cannot remember the call being placed. His daughter called Jake. He arrived after that.

We met Jake outside the main entrance to the hospital to comfort him and hug his girlfriend. The acknowledgment was not accepted. They pushed me out of the way, only concerned with our son. Looking back, understanding their intentions was just. However, a "brief" hug might have potentially built some strength for everyone. I let it go.

With everyone's attendance at the hospital, hours later, we were permitted to see him. With fear and apprehension, we entered the burn unit.

Cautiously peeking in each room to find him; some doctors called us over. They brought us into a large white room, exceedingly bright lights, and an individual lying on the hospital bed, which resembled a "mummy". It was my son. There was no visible appearance of his image, whatsoever. Any sign of a person was only; 2 small holes for eyes, the ventilation tube that protruded from the mouth, and tiny holes from each nostril.

Then the reality hit. I could feel "nothing", as tears poured endlessly from my eyes.

The doctors boldly described the situation at hand to us.

The severity of the damage, of being engulfed in flames, peeled off 80% of his body tissues. He was put into an induced coma to prevent shock to his brain and body. Numerous surgical procedures had to be performed to save his life. However, the case "we" give him a 1% chance of survival.

They gave me some papers to sign. My son was going to die.

I regained control with my shaking hands, and signed my name and left the unit. Not knowing what to do, neither where to go. My past thoughts of loneliness, abandonment, isolation, and being alone; came to me. But now, I felt utterly "alone", with no reason to live. When my son went, I was going too.

GODS ABSENCE

A brief period of mental blackout came over me inside the sizeable outdoor smoking area within the hospital's building. I sat there, smoked, and waited. Sitting alone in the dark, tears abundantly pouring to the cement, I could feel nothing. Dolly approached and grabbed me to her. As I leaned into her, my feelings regained. With her support, as always, her sincere act of warmth and kindness reached my heart. Collapsing in her strong arms; strengthened me.

With being able to comprehend this tragedy slightly, I prayed.

On my hands in knees, I screamed out loud for God's help. What his situation this bad? "I thought". Was this an accident, or was this a suicide attempt? Do we have a purpose in life, a destiny, or are we really "alone"? As I was praying, it began to hit me; "who in the hell am I talking to"?

There is no peace, calmness residing here. God wanted to kill my son. Vaguely recalling standing up at all due to the inability of muscle control, I was in a limbo state. Understanding the need to show strength for my daughter's sake, I regained my composure.

Standing straight up; eyes focused; being the soldier that was trained to handle volatile stress; I was now hysterically laughing uncontrollably. Dolly "knew" I had lost it.

THE PILL BOTTLE

Dolly grabbed my hand; "take these", she softly but firmly said.

Never had taken any medicine, except being treated for depression, one valium at age 16, and a few Tylenol periodically had no idea what was being offered. The bottle contained a large quantity of tiny little pills. When hesitantly inquiring about the effectiveness, I was told, "it would calm me down". She had explained to take one now, another before retiring for the night. Then tomorrow, if needed, take one every four hours; I agreed. We waited until I was mentally balanced, to go back to the burn unit, to say goodnight or goodbye.

The doctors had taken him to surgery, to perform the necessary procedure to save his life. That information was retrieved later. No memory after Dolly's conversation remains. That is only because; "five" pills were consumed, during our conversation, instead of one. She had no idea.

The next morning, a call was placed to the hospital. My son, still in surgery, critical condition, but still alive. There was nothing but to wait. Recognizing the importance, not to be buried alive in debt, went to work. I was responsible for making sure the dogs had sufficient food/water, the school was contacted, and I proceeded with the day. The desperate attempt to handle this crisis failed.

Recognizing the inability to gain emotional control was asked to "please", go be with my son. I did. To effectively gain solid control of my emotions, cope with the severe anxiety, take several pills, and then drive to the hospital.

Upon arriving, attempting to see him, I wished I had taken several more.

Numerous surgical procedures were done to save my son's life. Still wrapped from head to toe, with no visual evidence of his body, was now on complete life support. The induced coma remained to prevent shock to his brain. The machines, devices, and sounds; overwhelmed my senses. A multitude of tubes, wires, and needles protruded from his body. I stayed 10 minutes, to pray for him, and then left. Seeing my son's eyes shut, not knowing where he was, nor the outcome of this tragedy, unable to remain calm. I drove home, managed the dogs, studied my assignments for school, and took a few pills, retired for the night. With eyes pinned open, waiting for a call.

CRITICAL COMA

With the necessity of maintaining school progress, my sleep time was brief.

After calling the hospital, my son's status confirmed; 1% to live, critical, more surgeries needed.

However, he was still alive.

Overdue bills mounting by the day gave me the responsible reason to go to work. The dogs' needs were met, and I left. The only memories that day were; repetitious beeps of machines, hospital intercoms, and my son; all of which consumed my thought. Arriving later that evening at the hospital, I received more information about his status. More surgeries had been performed, as well as skin graphing to protect his bones and organs. A considering decision, to amputate the left arm, would be made soon. Still, he was given a slight chance to survive. My visit lasted 10 minutes, long enough for goodnights and prayers. This was utterly unbearable for me to see him like this. I went home, mechanically repeating my sequence of life. My arrival home was worsened, as; the water had been shut off due to an unpaid bill. That evening I prayed, hard.

Days and nights agonizingly crept slowly, ending with one week's recovery. My son remained in an induced coma.

LOOKING FOR FAITH

I have experienced many things in my life that I believed would break my spirit, but never anything like this. Believing if my son wouldn't survive through this ordeal, neither would I. My prayers were becoming more sincere to God, and my faith in God was becoming stronger.

The fact that I was not going to give up on my son was my "only" hope.

I continued to pray for him, knowing deep in my heart that was the only resource that I had. The hospital my son was in was extremely reputable, but I knew that exercising my faith now was of the utmost importance.

His 1% chance of living became higher, as each week passed. With the demanding schedule at hand, sleep was no longer becoming an option. Working, the dogs, house maintenance, school, and driving 75 miles a day to visit my son was starting to take a toll on me. It was mentally and physically challenging. I was becoming a pill-induced zombie. Sheer terrifying nightmares haunted me every night and into the day hours.

Maintaining two hours of sleep at night became the new norm.

I would have to say the worst feeling experienced was having to see my son's eyes closed and not knowing where he was; or what the realistic outcome of this tragic event would unfold. With every week that passed, my prayers were of less frequency. My faith was crumbling, as my God seemed to cease to exist as far as I was concerned. How could God allow this to happen? My guilt, pain, fears, despair magnified itself daily within the core of my soul.

I was allowing my life to be destroyed.

I could not figure out why this was happening to me.

The months rolled by, and most of the time was a blur in my mind.

Mainly because of the method of my survival was solely based on pharmaceutical medication. I was handling the situation calmly.

Primarily because I was strongly overmedicated all the time.

One evening after work, I had arrived at the hospital as usual. There were several doctors close to his bed; of course, I was expecting the worse. Courageously I walked toward my son, and to my surprise, his eyes were slightly open.

I collapsed.

DEATH ARRIVES

The following morning as I was preparing for work, the phone rang.

It was my mom. She asked if I was okay. Of course, I was fine, why wouldn't I be. My mother repeated herself. Again, I said, "Yes, what's up"? She said, "Danny's gone". I thought to myself, "Now where has he run off to"? I asked where she thought my son might be. She again repeated herself, "he's gone". The comprehension of what my mother was saying was not being understood.

I told her to stop playing and asked her what was going on. Finally, the words were said, "He's dead". She started crying. My heart stopped beating.

My breathing had stopped; I felt a strange piercing in my stomach. Then it seemed like, as I can only describe, a jagged butcher knife was stabbing me in my chest and ripping my organs out, all at once. Through the confusion and disbelief, I knew in my heart he was gone.

His presence in my spirit was not there.

I cried uncontrollably as I bashed my body against the wall and floor.

The next memory I have was collapsing in the corner, curling up like a fetus, and I, with my son, died too.

My heart broke into a million pieces. I was not aware of my surroundings, nor did I care. When I finally was able to stand, after a few hours, I could feel nothing. My love, my best friend, my confidant, my child, was taken from me. The God that I had always trusted and loved from childhood had betrayed me. The only thoughts

I had were how I was I going to live without him. The other was how I was going to get even with God.

It was a closed casket funeral, with a private viewing.

Evan and Dolly walked me down the aisle to see my son. As I approached his casket, memories, good and bad, were flashbacking in my mind.

When I could see him from a distance, my legs locked on me. I could not go through with this! This was going to kill me. Moving in slow motion towards him, I could see his face. As I stepped on the stool to kiss him, I felt the coldness of his skin, and knew at "that" time, that he was really gone. My heart was broken, and my faith was gone.

I hated God and was on a vengeance to destroy everything good.

MY BLACK HEART

My heart turned stone cold. I desired to have everyone around me dead. I thought of ways to take my own life. This would be something that I could never recover from. I made a promise to myself never to love again, never to feel nor to be happy and detached myself from everyone I knew.

The path of the road to my destruction was laid out. Little did I know that my demons were about to be unleashed again.

Continuing with my prescription addiction, my numbness grew with magnitude. I was teaching myself never to feel again. I hated my life. My partner and his addictions didn't help either. I learned to conceal my feelings and my pain from everyone.

I was learning not to remember anything bad in my life. I was losing all will to live any healthy life.

The pain was too great to bear anymore.

My greatest desire in life now was doing everything that I could to get back at my God! My daily thoughts consumed me of why; a God of love could take my son from me. I hated God, and then I hated myself more for these feelings.

As the next few years passed slowly, "all" I cared about was the pills, because I could zone out, and at least deal with being alive. The pharmaceutical medication became my "new God".

It was my strength, my love, my hope, and functioning without them was impossible. Evans' health was starting to deteriorate, and he passed away. So now I was alone again, "alone, alone", with just me and my pills.

When you are the only person in a room, day after day, you tend to think a lot. Financially I was doing okay. I even had a notion to start to believe in something again, possibly. Maybe it was the loneliness that stirred this desire, or just being tired of being unhappy. It was a little thought, but it was allowing me to feel something again slightly. The decision to start praying again was done out of desperation more or less, not love.

My life was filled with painful memories. So I continued to use the medication daily. My habit was up to $200 to $300 a week. Sometimes, even more than that, depending on where I had to obtain it.

ENDLESS PAIN

Several months passed by and my life seemed stable, because I was financially capable of being independent, for the longest time. I had endured "so" much these past few years, and I was still breathing.

Although taking my life was becoming an option. My sons' absence made me want to take my own life. At times, I felt as though I was dying on the inside. Looking back, I was slowly dying of a broken heart indeed.

Evan's absence didn't bother me that much because he was just my pill supplier. He had his issues as well. Our relationship was not one built on love. Instead, it mostly revolved around arguments.

Well, life was about to change "again". This time, I was unprepared. As I had started praying again to God, assuming that He would help me feel better about myself, I guess that idea waved bye-bye a long time ago.

Maybe when I prayed, God didn't hear, or I wasn't praying the correct way. Maybe just maybe there was "no" God because my life was getting ready to take a turn for the worse.

Right? Like it could get worse than this?

I had moved closer to my job. However, it didn't matter, because the establishment, where I had worked as a bartender, switched over management, and my job was taken after 9 years of employment. That wasn't so bad, because a freak accident one evening after work left my car totaled beyond repair. With only liability insurance, I tossed it as a complete loss.

Therefore "no" car, "no" job, I could not afford to live where I was renting a room from. I had one month to prepare myself for what my next move would be.

Quite frankly, I was ready to throw in the towel. Now I, with no doubt in my mind, believed God not only hated me but was doing everything He could to kill me.

I saw no end to the misery my God was putting me through. Since I had turned my back on Him over 30 years ago, this was what I deserved. Looking in the mirror was not an option for me anymore. Pure hatred, sadness, and despair were the only emotions looking back at me with those small black eyes. There was "no" soul left, no emotion, nothing. I had died. I was ashamed and felt as though I had not one person left in this world that loved me.

I had taken myself away from my immediate family only to protect them from seeing me like this. For many years I had done this, only not to hurt them.

My pain and my demons were surrounding me at an ever-increasing pace. I would periodically call my family to let them know that I was still alive but always lied by telling them things were great.

INTENTIONAL DISTANCE

My daughter and her husband were thrilled with their first child. The little girl was given the same name as my son, only a more feminine version. My mother was starting to get up there in age; however, she could still do circles around all of us. I had made a promise to myself, for my loved ones to not see me like this. My abusive pill addiction was taking control of my life and my mind. I loved my family so much; I could not bear for them to be concerned with me. I was becoming so tired. Peace had left me a long, long time ago. Missing having a relationship with my family was starting to tear at my heart. It was one week before I had to move. I was finalizing where my personal belongings were going to be stored. Having no location to go and honestly not caring what happened to me, I started to give up. My pill intake was being drastically reduced for the first time in six years. I was having frequent withdrawal symptoms due to my inability to support my habit.

The only good thoughts that I had at the time were that of my son. It appeared as if I was starting to come to terms with his passing. The realization came to mind that my grief was subsiding with time. That, I "was" grateful for. I cried occasionally, but it seemed as time was going by, I was healing.

Without having an overload of medication in my system, I was starting to think more clearly. I was starting to become fed up with my life. I was tired of being sick. I was tired of being depressed. I was tired of not feeling worthy. I was tired of being alone. Most of all, I was tired of "NOT FEELING" Period!

JESUS HEAR ME

One evening, alone in my bed, I was withdrawing really bad from my medication. It had been days since my last fix. I could not sleep at all. I was tossing and turning, and I started to pray to God. As I was beginning to dismantle my sheets with my body, a thought hit me. Small at first, but it began to grow inside my mind. When I was a child, and I was scared and couldn't sleep, I talked to a friend. It was Jesus.

I kept thinking of Him, and my thoughts started to consume me. Tears poured from my eyes until I could no longer breathe. With deep sincerity, I asked Him to help me.

Without concern, I asked Him to please use me once again. I had nothing more to lose in life. Out of despair, I asked Him to give me "a reason to live", forgetting all about "this" book I started from years prior. Wanting to forget the past, pressing on in my prayer, incredible energy came over my body. From the top of my head to my toes, it felt like a slow-moving electric current wave.

My tears that had drenched my pillows immediately dried from my eyes. For the first time in a very long time, peace was felt in my heart. There was a calmness in my spirit, which I can only describe as pure love. As I opened my eyes and raised my head, my attention was drawn to a massive picture frame that my daughter gave me the previous Christmas. It was filled with pictures of her family. The one that got my attention was my granddaughter. That adorable face that could thaw a room full of ice touched my heart. What happened in the next few seconds was an awakening, and only I can describe it as a small miracle. I think God heard me.

It had been many years, six years to be exact, that I actually had felt my body. There seemed to be a spark of hope in my heart that maybe I could somehow get this terrible habit broken. But doing it alone was impossible. Maybe I did need help. Maybe I needed Jesus.

ROCK BOTTOM

A week passed, I moved out of my house. I had no car, no income, nowhere to live, and a $300 a week methadone habit. By now, I was using ecstasy and cocaine, which was taking another $50 to $100 a day. So, you can do the math. It does not take a rocket scientist to know where that money was collected from. My self-esteem was being ripped me because I had no choice in the matter. On the other hand, I was being taken advantage of by other people because of my situation. Everything in my life was making me sick. Even the people I thought were my friends deserted me and treated me like I was an insignificant human being. Guess it is true what they say about money and friends. If you have money, you will always have friends.

I tried to stop taking the pills and using the cocaine, but the addiction had taken over.

The damage had been done.

ALONE ALONE

One month passed by, and there was no income coming in. I was renting a room above a liquor store. The owner was my previous employer. He owned several businesses in the area. I had applied for unemployment, and that was obtainable.

It was something; however, the wait for benefits was another month. So I waited.

I had five months to look for a job.

Winter was creeping up fast. It was November; cold weather was starting to set in. So was my loneliness.

My best friend had suddenly passed away from a heart attack.

He was the only transportation that I had. My other, only friend turned her back on me. She was the main supplier of my methadone habit, along with two other gentlemen, that were selling me their ridiculous price of pills. The only life that I had was watching movies while I chained smoked in the dark, in my 10' by 12' bedroom. My cash intake was at such a bare minimum that there were days I went without. I was sick from withdrawals most of the nights. I remember a friend telling me, "When you have a problem, run "to" God, not "away". So, I prayed.

Didn't know if God heard me, so I talked to my friend Jesus. Since God turned His back, I tried to trust Jesus.

I had lost all hope in any future. Therefore, I just waited every day to die. I had no reason to live anymore, and I gave up. I was alone. But I still talked to Jesus. Every night, I talked to Him, crying, telling Him

I wanted to be with Him, because I was just "so" tired of living in this much pain, every day, day after day.

Watching movies all day, and part of the night was becoming a real bore. I had remembered several years ago, starting to write this autobiography. Figuring that I had nothing else to occupy time with, the desire to write again became an option. I stayed alone in my room, withdrawing from my medicine, no food, and very little heat.

My computer, my pen, my paper, and my life, and my ever seeing cigarette falling from my mouth, was my life. For days on end, I wrote.

After a while, I started to have lucid dreams of my past—fond memories and lingering nightmares that awoke me in the middle of the night, sweating. So I prayed and talked to Jesus. I didn't know how to pray, but as a child, I remembered Jesus as my only friend. I started to gain a bit of hope. Then something happened.

THE HOSPITALIZATION

My mother, which had been in the hospital for having a heart valve surgery replacement, had a huge setback. She had to be put on a ventilator because she had stopped breathing after the surgery.

This was the same hospital where my son had been admitted to during his ordeal with the fire accident. So, it was tough for me to go to her.

But I did. Earlier, my daughter called to tell me to get up there immediately because she had stopped breathing. She didn't know exactly what was happening, nor could she give me any more information. I didn't know what to expect. I couldn't go through this again. My mind couldn't handle it.

SICK AND TIRED

As I peeked through the curtain at the hospital, lying on the bed was my mother. She was bloated from the Lasik and was unconscious.

The sight of her brought back too many memories. My family was there and crying in front of them was not an option. After a few minutes, everyone went downstairs. I laid hands on my mother and prayed for her.

Ironically, my faith seems to appear when there are others that I love concerned. In my heart, I have always cared more for others than myself. My addictions never allowed me to show it properly. Being a few days clean, it was tough for me to be there.

As I finished praying, everyone came back upstairs from lunch. My mother had slightly opened her eyes as I was speaking to her. There was a sparkling light beaming from her eyes.

That was my next awakening. Since I had been off the pills and cocaine for three days, the numbness was wearing off, and my senses were coming back. It was at that time, after realizing that my mother might not make it through this surgery, how short and how precious life really is. Upon making my way out of the hospital, I stopped to call my pill connection. She refused to help me because of my lack of funds. Looking back, it was probably the best response that she had ever given me.

Unfortunately for me, my shaking lasted all the way home. When I arrived home, I collapsed, and then I prayed. This time I was utterly helpless indeed. Since my so-called friend that had been my supplier of pills deserted me.

I had no money. Therefore, my other connections failed me. I was hungry.

I was tired. I was fed up! This time I prayed to God in the name of Jesus.

I didn't know how to talk to God. Therefore I tried everything. I pleaded to God that I wanted my life back. In that instance, the decision was made. "I am done", "it is over, I give up", I screamed to my God!

There were many sleepless nights the week that preceded that prayer. My withdrawals were terrifying but were necessary to become clean again.

It was disturbing and unusually painful.

I had restless leg syndrome. For those who do not know, it is where your feet and especially your legs can not remain still. I prayed that it would not last long. My voice had become hoarse from cursing at my family and my friends, my employer, and even the strangers I had spoken to outside. The only difference was that this time, my only friend was Jesus. I had no choice but to rely on Him this time. I had "nothing", and "nobody". My 10' by 12' unheated room, no food, no hope, no love. Just God and my prayers. I was starting to realize that maybe He might hear me and figure out what to do, to take this pain away. I was "so" tired.

IM PRAYING WHERE ARE YOU?

Thoughts were starting to come to me days after, that punishing God, by destroying His creation, would not bring my son back. Killing myself would not mend my relationship with my family because my presence would not be. I was beginning to feel slightly better after a few weeks. It was put in my heart to proceed with writing again. My cocaine habit was still intact, but guilty thoughts haunted me every day, as I still used. Even though I was still using, the desperate need to stop burned in me. I was still living inside of a bubble.

Seeing the world and touching, but not being able to feel anything and not telling anyone how I felt. So, I kept writing every day out of boredom, and I kept praying to God for help.

Over the next few weeks, life seemed to be about the same, except my food supply seemed to last longer than before. But there again, peanut butter and jelly can go a long way.

Sometimes I just put two pieces of bread together and used my imagination. Then, of course, let's not forget seafood night on the weekends. What I saw was what I got!

I was becoming a writing fool. Sometimes I was awake at 3:00 am typing away. I would sit there for hours on end, cigarette hanging from my mouth, and snorting a few lines of coke every so often. After a few weeks, even the powder was losing its flair. It was making me feel so guilty, as I was trying to get myself together. Therefore, I prayed about it. Before I had realized, my praying had become almost a ritual every night.

What else did I have anyway?

Besides, the sincerity that I felt in my heart was real. Even if God didn't hear me, I meant it this time. Knowing deep down inside in my heart that I loved Jesus, I decided to trust Him once again. I professed to Him, with my mouth once more, that He is Christ, and I give my heart back to Him and trust Him with my life.

Little did I realize in my wildest dreams and imagination what events were about to occur in my life. That indeed was about to change my life forever. The experiences of a lifetime that were the most painful and beautiful memories of my life, and I pray, will never forget. I was about to find out where "God" was all my life, and it wasn't in the sky.

GRATITUDE

My life was consisting of writing during the wee hours of the morning, until the late night. In the evenings, watching movies was my favorite pastime. A few long, winter weeks had passed. My mother was slowly recovering in a nursing home. She was to reside there briefly, only until she was more stabilized to come home. However, a slow recovery, she was quite better. I was happy my prayers were answered. I felt God might have heard me. But when was He going to be a part of my life again? I kept asking Him, but He never gave me an answer. So, I kept writing, wondering when He would hear my prayers for me. I guess He was quite mad at me for turning away from Him all my life. I pleaded with Him to help me feel again, "something, anything", I asked.

A RESISTABLE URGE

As my writing desire increased, I needed to edit it on the computer.

Reviewing my work, it had to start from the beginning of the book, my childhood. So, I guess this is where God started to do His thing. At least that is where I thought He was.

As I had to recall and face the past once again, nightmares began to surface more frequently.

I would wake up in the middle of the night, strong memories of the past. My life was being replayed in my mind, night after night. Terrifying dreams of my son replayed itself over and over. I was starting to remember my life, in direct order of my age progression, and everything and everyone that I had hurt over a lifetime. All of the damage that I had done to myself, my children, my friends, and my family, tore at my heart. Tears were rolling down my eyes, pouring into my pillows, as I realized how I had betrayed God. When I had realized this, it seemed as someone kicked my stomach in, and I doubled over in extreme pain.

A few hours passed; my crying never ceased. With my head buried in my pillows, in shame, and fear, I covered myself with my sheets, and I tried to hide from God. I was so embarrassed and humiliated even to pray anymore. Even writing was not an option anymore. My dreams at night and my memories seemed to consume my every thought.

Every night there was a new chapter in my life to remember. There was a different twist, though. Even during "all" of the bad times I recalled, my life seems to get somehow pulled back the right way.

There was always something "there" getting me through the rough times. It seemed as when my life was hanging on by thin string; "something or someone" helped me get back on the right track. But I had no clue what it was. I just wanted to know why I was being punished and why God disliked me so much. But I still loved Him.

AN ANGEL OF MERCY

One night was especially rough on me. I had been crying most of the day, for no apparent reason. Guilt and extreme remorse were killing me and tearing me up on the inside. I prayed, of course, still waiting for God to help me. I closed my eyes and began to pray. Something was stirring in me, but no clue what was about to happen to me.

I had a vision and saw a dimmed outline of a person, dressed in all white, covered from the head down to his feet.

There was no evidence of a body, just an illuminating light surrounding it everywhere. I was not scared, and the light did not hurt my eyes. Looking back now, I believe my thought was, "I'm dying". I was happy because my pain in my heart was ceasing. Then, my next thought was, "I'm hallucinating". The drugs were gone, so that wasn't right either. The last resort of analytical thinking was, "I had finally lost my mind". However, it felt good!

Stretching out my hand to this person seemed to be my only desire. So I did. Now, I will explain as clearly possible what I had felt after that. Take every happy moment that you have ever felt in your entire life, every joyous feeling your mind can imagine, and multiply that 100 times.

That couldn't come close to what I was feeling. The peace and contentment that was felt were indescribable. Beyond even that was the most powerful sense of love and security, I had "EVER" experienced in my life. You could not buy these feelings that I had experienced that night. I felt safe beyond any rational thought could ever conjure up. I thought I was dead. To be honest with you, if this was death. Let's roll on up out of here!

I believe the experience lasted a few minutes. My arm let go, and my mind had to let go of the experience, because of the intensity of emotion that I was feeling. If it makes any sense, it was "too" good to be real.

When my prayer session was over, I could not make any rational decisions about what just happened to me.

However, my peace of mind was there that night, and the crying stopped, at least for the night. "Maybe I had found God again"; I thought to myself.

The next few days were rough because I still had terrible memories. I had put off what I had experienced, believing still, why God would have anything to do with me. I wanted His help and continued to pray. He showed up.

THE FINAL BATTLE WITH GOD

I continued to work diligently on this autobiography, despite the ongoing nightmares that were experienced every night. There seemed to be a presence with me, however. I assumed my demons were starting to creep up on me again. The mental pain that was being barely endured was keeping me up every night. It was almost impossible for me to continue writing. I still prayed nightly and asked God to please help me find peace in my mind. Then, I would swear to Him and cry to Him as to why He was punishing me and why He took my son from me. There were answers to questions that needed to be answered. So every night, I had it out with God. I wanted to know why a God, my God, that I loved so much and still believed in, "still", had betrayed me.

Well, when I got finished telling "God" about "Himself", after endless weeks of no sleep; "He" told me about "myself".

In my room, cold, no food, family, friends, money; He showed up. Only to my surprise after 40 years, He "never" left. It was I that betrayed Him.

One terrible evening it was put in my heart to review some pictures of unborn babies in the womb as they progressed with time. A picture caught my eye for some reason. It was an aborted fetus, with its limbs torn apart. This is where God started to tear my heart and pull me back to Him.

Remembering an abortion I had when I was 15 and had forgotten about this made me realize that I had killed my child. The remorse and guilt was just the beginning of my purging from God. I couldn't sleep for three weeks. In this time of shame, I realized "all" my life I have had choices. It was me that left my God, my faith, my first love.

Then I knew how much I still loved Jesus. He was "always" there.

Nothing will ever compare, nor ever will to how much shame I felt in the core of my spirit. I was shown every sin that came to remembrance, and sin that was lost in time.

Even acts that were not even thought of as sins, God revealed to me. The more that was recalled, it made me wonder why I had made these awful decisions. I had loved and accepted Christ as a child.

Even as an adult, I reconfirmed my faith by accepting Christ as my Savior again. But the problem was I never followed Him, by His rules. I kept praying for faith, truth, wisdom, and understanding. I asked to see myself and what I had become. God showed up.

THE TRUTH REVEALED

The point of absolute misery and discontentment haunted my every waking hour. Had I really strayed this far from God, my whole life? My face remained buried in my pillows each night, drenched with tears. My ability to face God anymore was impossible. I was immobilized with fear because my God, my Father in Heaven, finally showed up. However, it was only for me to discover the harsh reality that He never left me. He allowed me to make my own decisions in life.

He allowed me to be deceived by the enemy.

He was there in the midst of "all" my trials. He stood by me while I made mistake after mistake. He held my hand when I was scared. He prevented me numerous times from taking my life. It was Him who put those little thoughts of encouragement in my spirit. It was Him who fed me when I was hungry, clothed me, and kept me warm when I was cold.

It was Him who picked me up and prevented me from dying when my son died.

He had turned His back because; "I" threw Him out of my life and "my" heart. How could I bear living with this?

HE NEVER LEFT

When I realized what I had done to Him, and deeply sorry I was, I gave Him my whole heart once more. For the first time in my life, I, 100% let go and gave God complete control. I am completely done, and I trust you completely with my life. Knowing truthfully, I didn't want the responsibility anymore. Then something happened.

The remorse and guilt and pain started to subside gradually. The nightmares were decreasing, almost disappearing overnight.

I cried every night when I prayed, but something was different. Even though my loneliness was felt most of the time, I didn't feel alone anymore. I knew Jesus was right beside me. Praying all the time, hours a night was starting to have an impact on my life. I prayed to learn the proper way to pray. I prayed for the Holy Spirit. I prayed to be close to God. I prayed for help.

My family was not there, and my friends had deserted me. Most of the time, I just prayed because it felt unnatural for me not to.

My praying became so intense that I started having lucid dreams and visions. I prayed to God to send me other Christians to help me, and I also prayed for a church.

LOOKING FOR FELLOWSHIP

The place where I lived had a church right across the street from me. Knowing this, I never went, but something kept catching my eye and my spirit. Months went by; my dreams and visions remained nightly. I continued to pray and remain diligent as I read my bible every day. There was still something missing. The desire to be around other children of God was making my heart bleed. Every day, as I walked by the church, I looked intensely. I knew I wanted to find a church, however, could it have been that obvious, so right in my face, that I couldn't see it there?

I made a few phone calls to various churches, trying to get one that I might like to go to.

One Saturday afternoon walking back from getting a soda, I literally froze in my tracks, my head turned at the church across from me. "Go," The Holy Spirit said. "Now"? I replied. "Go!" My spirit insisted! Before I knew it, I was walking across the street, into the parking lot, entering inside.

When I went in, a gentleman with the kindest eyes and the gentlest smile I had seen in a very long time greeted me. Asking for information about the church, all I needed to know was, if they believed in the Holy Trinity. They did.

I showed up for the 10:30 Sunday service. Satan and his vile mutants tried everything to prevent me from going. My pantyhose ripped, and I had a minimal choice of clothes to wear. My hair was acting stupid, and I almost fell going down the stairs. God said, "go as you are". I did.

Within 10 minutes of listening to the Bishop preach his sermon, I knew that The Holy Spirit had brought me here. At the end of the service, I knew that God had placed me here to be a member of this church.

With the Bishops open arms around me and hugging me as I came forward, I was overwhelmed because it had been a long time since I had felt that unconditional love. God was here too! The next day I found a job after five months of being unemployed. The dreams and visions stopped.

MY REASON TO LIVE

It was April 26th, 2015 that I joined my new church. During the early months, all I could do was cry. It wasn't because I was broke, it wasn't because I had no car, it wasn't because I lost everything I had and was living above a liquor store.

It was because my God, my father, my King, my love, allowed me to lose "all" these worldly possessions to show me that He was "always there" and He "always" loved me, even when I hated Him, He still loved me. I cry because it was "I" that asked Him to be my God again. He has shown me how to trust Him through faith and His Word.

He has split my heart down to nothing and is rebuilding it with concrete and love. For the first time in my life, I can feel. I never knew what real unconditional love felt like before.

This is why I "can" cry.

There is no more pain.

There is no more shame. There is no more guilt. I know now what it means to be buried with Christ on the cross. I also know that the enemy has been deceiving me my whole life and had taken everything from me. He has taken my sanity, family, heart, love for Christ, and almost my life.

Over eight years ago, I started to write this autobiography. I was under the assumption that the book was going to be a self-help book about alcoholism and recovery. I was hoping to get a few copies for my family, friends, and myself. Now I know the real reason. This book was never about "me". Instead, it was my testimony, and I never realized it.

This book was "all" about God. It was to give Him Glory. It was to show you His power and His love. Even when we hate Him, He still loves us. When I was running from Him, He followed beside me. When I was hurting, He picked me and held me. When I finally gave up, He took me back into His arms, like I was never gone.

What can match "any "love like that?

I will never deny Jesus Christ again, ever! When I need Him, all I have to do is believe. I know He is with me, and I know how much He loves us.

I believe by faith; He is only beginning with me. I want all of this filth taken from me. If "you" give your life to Him, you "will" be healed. Listen to me. I have made many mistakes in my life. I have suffered many losses and much pain. My next 50 years will be enjoyed by taking back my life. I will continue to pray for others that are broken and left for dead. It is my quest to make the enemy tremble, with Christ's Power in me, through prayer. I know I will be attacked, but know I have the full armor of God and a multitude of angels around me. I have never been alone. Glory to God!

My Father, My King, as I bow my head to you on my knee, I dedicate this book to you, My Friend, my Creator. You are my "Reason to Live", and my reason to die. Glory to God!

The End

Back in love with my God. The End So now, today, it is January 25th, 2016. My 53rd birthday just passed on January 16th. Ironic numbers, I must add. Today I have been sober for 21 years. My addiction to pharmaceutical products and cocaine has been surrendered to Christ.

I am over one year clean. Since last May of 2015, I started to pray about my smoking habit that I have had since I was 12 years old. I had asked God to take away the urge to smoke. I knew I could never accomplish such a task by myself. But, it was in my heart, to "believe" God could. When I said that, I put down my last cigarette. Today, it has been six months since I have been delivered from a 40-year habit.

I had to pause writing this because I have tears rolling down my cheeks. Only a God of love can do this.

As I try every day to walk by the Spirit, and most of the time, it is not easy. I am constantly under spiritual attack by the enemy.

However, I am learning to use the Power of The Holy Spirit to teach me to fight. When I pray, it is for hours on end. I intervene for many people, as my job lets me contact other Christians who give me their prayer requests. Somehow, someway I always seem to end up with talking to the right people. Well, no, God sends them to me. That's my Daddy!

I have let the past go. I have let my son go. He is with God now. As much as I miss him, I am at peace with that.

I read my bible daily and try humbly to follow "all" of God's 10 Commandments. I tithe weekly to my church for God's work. I serve in church whenever I am needed. I dress more conservatively and modestly. My repentance daily is done at night. I can no longer sin against my God and not feel shame.

In return, what He has done for me and to me is priceless.

I am no longer the same person.

My purging takes place daily. I asked to be changed rapidly, and I assume the answer to that prayer was "yes". Today I am grateful to be back with Him. Today I am back in love with my God!